ROCK-N-ROLL

TREASURES

IDENTIFICATION
& VALUE GUIDE

Joe Hilton
Greg Moore

cb

COLLECTOR BOOKS

A Division of Schroeder Publishing Co., Inc.

On the cover:

Yellow Submarine Goebel figurines, 1968, West Germany
The Monkees vinyl lunchbox and thermos, 1968, US, mfg. by Thermos; lunchbox., $300.00 – 400.00, thermos, $75.00 – 125.00.
The Beatles ceramic vase, UK, 1963, $1,000.00 – 1,500.00.
The Banana Splits game, US, 1969, Hasbro, $500.00 – 600.00.
Elvis Presley Rock-N-Roll guitar, 1956, EPE, $1,500.00 – 2,000.00.
Chuck Berry personally owned and signed guitar, $4,000.00 – 6,000.00.
KISS comic book, US, Marvel Comics, $35.00 – 45.00.
Madonna TV Guide, US, $25.00 – 30.00.

Cover design by Beth Summers
Book design by Joyce Cherry

Searching For A Publisher?

We are always looking for knowledgeable people considered to be experts within their fields. If you feel that there is a real need for a book on your collectible subject and have a large comprehensive collection, contact Collector Books.

Collector Books
P.O. Box 3009
Paducah, Kentucky 42002-3009

Copyright © 1999 by Joe Hilton & Greg Moore

Contents

Dedication

This book is dedicated to my wife Marilyn, my daughter Jessica, and my parents
Clyde and Gladys for all their love and guidance.
Joe Hilton

This book is dedicated to my wife, Pam.
Greg Moore

Acknowledgments

We would like to thank the following people for their valuable contributions to this book:

Mark and Tracy Abrams
Jeff Augsburger
Sue Bradford
Beth Brightbill
Greg Byxbee
Fred Carlson
Ed Chernesky
Kit Close/Ranch Records
Jacqueline Cortes
Paul Costanzo
Dennis and Connie Dailey
Roy Damm IV
Tom and Mary Fontaine

Randy French
David Fuqua
Steve Fymbo
Jim Gambino
Joe Gornall
Bob Gottuso
Tom Haack
David Harper
Gary Lance
Chris Philip
Rock n' Hollywood, Las Vegas
Scott Seavers
Kip Siess

Bari Smalley
Fred Tweedie/Oasis Records
Bill Weaver
Dale Wettstein
Marc and Debra Zakarin

A very special thanks to the following individuals:

Ron Beauchamp
Phil Biebl
Frank Caiazzo
Perry Cox
Gary Conn Jr.
Bob Esch
Krista Fenstad
Brian and Stephanie Fischer

Tony Fornaro
Mike Fox
Barb Garten
Anthony George
Don and Debi Hunter
Jeff Kline
Patti Ledoux
Diane May

Sheryl Mennes
Carmine Milicia
Mark Naboshek
Wayne Rogers
Michelle Ruelas
Collin Weaver

Preface

Rock-n-Roll Treasures is the most complete and accurate identification and price guide for rock-n-roll music memorabilia ever assembled to date. The easy-to-read format chronicles over 40 years of the rarest rock-n-roll collectibles known to exist. This book presents over 2,000 pieces of rock memorabilia from nearly 100 rock-n-roll artists, including many artifacts that have never appeared in print before. Extensive chapters on The Beatles, concert memorabilia, autographed items, instruments, and one-of-a-kind rock items are featured. This information has been compiled over several years by top experts in the field. Each chapter contains a written background followed by a listing of items produced including detailed descriptions and current market values. Our society has been tremendously affected by the music we call rock-n-roll. Since the early days of Buddy Holly, Elvis Presley, and the Beatles, these and other rock-n-roll superstars have formed the foundation of the music industry as it is today. The music memorabilia generated from rock-n-roll stars is vast and could never be completely cataloged, however we have assembled a substantial amount of the rarest rock-n-roll collectibles known to exist.

About the Authors

Collecting has always been a fun hobby for Joe. In the 1960s he collected stamps and coins, comic books, model kits, and baseball cards. Growing up with two teenage girls next door who loved The Beatles helped spark his love for this remarkable band. He watched the Saturday morning Beatles cartoons with them and spent time listening to their Beatles records. Later, he took an interest in antiques and collectibles and after finishing college became aware of the growing interest in rock-n-roll music memorabilia. He began attending record shows and Beatles conventions in the 1970s and soon became immersed in building a rock-n-roll memorabilia collection of his own. If you have Beatles items for sale, please contact Joe at 603-332-5770.

As a member of the Banana Splits fan club in 1968, Greg's love for music grew. In 1969 he began collecting record albums of all kinds of music. With a growing appreciation for music, Greg enrolled in broadcasting. After a short time The Music Man, a successful mobile disc-jockey business was born. Greg ran this business through the late 1980s. In 1986 while attending a toy show with his family, Greg became aware of the vast array of rock-n-roll collectibles other than records. Soon afterward he bought his first trinket, an Elvis Presley doll. A serious hobby arose from this. This is Greg's third book on collectibles.

Introduction

Valuing Memorabilia

The single most important thing to remember when using this book is that the price ranges given serve only as a guideline. The value of any item is exactly what someone is willing to pay for it. Much of the escalation in memorabilia pricing is due to publication of trade price guides which depict prices sometimes high and sometimes low. The difficult task for collectors has always been which sources to believe. It seems that to decide the value of an item, a person has to consult many sources. One thing's for sure: it's always profitable if one can double one's money which is at the very least what many people do when investing in the toy market. Not only is it wise to buy items at low prices but also to be selective with your purchases. By keeping this in mind and by accurately grading an item's condition, it's hard to go wrong. Many items in this book, especially the rarer items, will continue to climb in price as time goes on. These pieces have always proven to be a good investment. It's important to note that many of the items displayed in this book only escalate in value due to demand. This factor alone will determine the destiny of today's rock-n-roll treasures. How could one go wrong with purchasing a Jimi Hendrix vintage stage outfit or a Buddy Holly personally owned guitar?

Grading an Item's Condition

Nothing is more important than an item's condition, period. Rarity also plays an important role. The seasoned collector knows the importance of quality and will pass by most items that aren't in top condition. A beginning collector may purchase items in most any condition to start building a collection. As collectors become more educated and informed, they may choose to upgrade an item because of condition. This is common practice. The following grading guidelines are considered to be the universal grading system adopted by collectors and memorabilia dealers worldwide.

All values presented in this book are for items in the top grades, i.e., excellent to mint condition.

Grading Guidelines:

☆ Grade 10 – Mint Condition. Perfect condition. If included, the box, card, or package must also be perfect. Items in mint condition are in the best possible condition; these items cannot be upgraded. Note: Brand new store-bought items may not be mint due to handling or manufacturer flaws.

☆ Grade 9 – Near Mint Condition. Extremely slight (usually shelf) wear. If boxed or carded, item may have been removed and returned to packaging but not played with or used substantially. Item has a like-new appearance.

☆ Grade 8 – Excellent Condition. Minor wear but item still displays well with no major flaws. Original packaging may have slight wear or minor crease. Grades 8 and above are the best to collect for resale investment.

☆ Grade 7 – Very Good Condition. Items definitely show wear, fading possible, shows use but still complete. Original packaging may have slight damage (corner splits, small tears, damaged cellophane).

☆ Grade 6 – Good Condition. Items have considerable wear: scratches, worn paint, chips, or missing decals. Parts may be missing. Original packaging has considerable damage as well. These items may display heavy writing, staining, or be badly crushed. Avoid purchasing items in this or lower grades unless extremely rare. An item in good condition is usually valued at 40 – 50% of the Grade 10 value.

☆ Grades 5 through 1 – Poor through Bad Condition. This condition represents items in very poor to totally trashed condition. Only if the item is truly a rarity would someone purchase it in these conditions. An item in this condition range cannot be valued at more than 10 – 20% of Grade 10.

Note: original packaging, i.e., boxes, backing cards, etc., can usually account for 50 – 75% of an item's value.

Buying

Nothing is more exciting in the collectors' world than when he or she finds a great piece of memorabilia at an unbelievable price. This process is basically known as the thrill of the hunt. All you collectors know exactly what we're talking about here. After all those hours spent searching and tracking, it's really nice when it pays off! Patience is a virtue.

Many collectors seek certain specialty items like lunchboxes, Beatle collectibles, autographs, and one-of-a-kind items. When dealing with sellers, it is useful to ask them if they have exactly what you're looking for. Many sellers that you might deal with at a collectible show have more than they can display and have boxes of items hidden from view under tables. Additionally, by making contacts at shows you may stumble on a gold mine of memorabilia by merely trading phone numbers. Making and keeping good contacts is the key to building an impressive collection.

Be sure to thoroughly inspect all items you're considering for purchase. Many expensive mistakes are made when the buyer acts too hurriedly. Remember: Condition is everything! Once inspected, a value can then be accurately determined. Knowing values for items can also be important when making in-person transactions. For mail order and auctions, there's time to do your research before purchasing. Always ask for several photographs of any items you're considering.

Ask questions such as: "what's the history of this item?" If the seller has more than one of the item you want and they are affordable, buy them all for investment or for later trading. Some 1960s items surface occasionally in bulk. Knowing your product, current prices, and the rarity allows the collector to make a big find. Many warehouse finds of Beatles memorabilia from the 1960s have occurred: Beatle sneakers in original boxes, the Yellow Submarine Pop Out Art Decorations Book, Beatle 8" nodder dolls in original boxes, Beatle concert tickets, Beatle headbands in original unopened packages, Beatle licorice records with their cardboard store displays, Beatle headphones, Beatle wigs, Yellow Submarine stick-ons, switch plate covers, key chains, paint sets, and stationery sets. I'm sure there have been many others we've never heard about.

A last note on buying: watch out for reproductions. We have noted throughout this book all items that have known reproductions. Just be aware that many items have been counterfeited over the years and probably will continue to be. Most of these bootleg items can be distinguished from their authentic counterparts. Many items will be obvious while others will require careful examination. Just be aware.

Selling

Selling can also be a precarious experience. Before selling an item, always do your homework. Knowing how and where to sell rock-n-roll collectibles is as important as knowing how and where to buy them. Some rare items are very easy to sell but hard to give values. Always remember that an item's value is only what someone is willing to pay for it. Sometimes one gets top dollar for an item and other times not. Just be fair when selling your collectibles and be as honest as possible. In the long run, this formula will prove to be best. Trading items with others is sometimes a useful way of getting new items and reducing your overall costs. Creative and effective trading takes time and skill to master. As a seller it is wise to make as many contacts as you can. By talking with people and keeping lists of what buyers are looking for, the seller has an edge. It's always easier to buy if you know what to sell and to whom. Many clubs are available for rock-n-roll enthusiasts and are good avenues for contacts whether buying or selling. The more contacts you make, the broader your selection of sale items becomes. By using these guidelines you have a better chance of locating the items you want.

There are several ways to sell your collectibles today:

Auctions. These usually return the most money for rock-n-roll collectibles given an interested audience. Whether selling one item or an entire collection, the auction market place is a good choice. Make sure the auction you intend to utilize has a sufficient following for your items. Keep in mind not all items will bring top dollar. Establish reserve prices to protect your investment.

Trade Magazines. Many people place classified advertisements in national newspapers and magazines. This can be an effective means of selling your merchandise.

The Internet. The World Wide Web has recently proved to be a popular medium for both buying and selling rock-n-roll collectibles. Check out the particular Internet site before selling to ensure potential buyers and collectors frequent it.

Selling your entire collection to a collector and/or a dealer. Certainly selling your collection all at once to a collector would probably return the best price for your items. Finding a collector willing to purchase an entire collection is a task in itself. Advertising to all known contacts is the best approach here. If you are considering selling your collection to a dealer, keep in mind that the dealer probably at best would only offer you 50-60% of the market value. They are looking to resell your items and make a profit, but this avenue is often the quickest and fastest way to sell your collection.

Protecting Your Investment

Care should be taken to protect your rock-n-roll collectibles. Sunlight, humidity, and dust are key factors to consider when displaying your collection. They can all damage items if proper care is not exercised. Paper and other items should always be wrapped in mylar protected covers.

Photographs and videos of your collection should be taken and submitted with appraisals to your insurance company. You never know when a disaster might strike. Many insurance companies write special policies to cover collectibles and the price of these policies is relatively small when compared to the value of some collections.

Some collectors attempt to touch up the defects on their less than mint condition collectibles. A word to the wise ... don't. I once purchased a very rare Beatles Yellow Submarine wrist watch that had a scratched outer dial. At the time I paid a lot of money for it. I knew the dial was scratched but I knew once I bought the item I would simply replace the scratched outer dial with a new one. I contacted a watch repair shop and asked them if the dial could be easily replaced and they told me it shouldn't be a problem. I received the watch in the mail. It looked great but the dial was very scratched and worn so I proceeded to take the back off the watch. As soon as I took the back off, half the painted surface that pictured the Beatles on the watch face simply crumbled and fell off! Major devastation. My new watch went from a condition 7 to a condition 1 in half a second. A word to the wise — don't touch-up or alter your collectibles! One can usually tell when an item has been repainted, reglued, etc. Many collectors will not purchase an item that's in this condition. If you purchase collectibles like these and intend to resell them, it is imperative to mention these touch-ups when presenting your items for sale. Remember, honesty is the best policy!

With a little care and protection, your collection can be enjoyed for years to come.

The Top Ten

The Beatles

No rock-n-roll group had more influence on a generation and the world as The Beatles. They helped change the 1960s and their influence is still felt today. Music, culture, lifestyles, hairstyles, clothing styles, and attitudes all changed because of this remarkable band that emerged from Liverpool, England, in the early 1960s. The Beatles were John Lennon, Paul McCartney, George Harrison, and Ringo Starr.

The Beatles themselves were greatly influenced by the early rock-n-roll stars from America such as Elvis Presley, Fats Domino, Buddy Holly, Gene Vincent, and others. During the band's infancy they spent a considerable amount of time listening to and copying the styles of these great 1950s rock-n-roll heroes. It's fair to say that the music style adopted by the Beatles has its roots in 1950s American rock-n-roll.

The Beatles arrived on the music scene in the very early 1960s and by 1963 had established themselves as the premier rock-n-roll band in all of England. Frenzied crowds greeted the Beatles wherever they appeared throughout England. Beatlemania was born. The American music scene had all but ignored what was transpiring in England. But by January 1964 following the release of the Beatles second album in England, America could no longer resist the onslaught of these four lovable guys with mop-top haircuts.

They stormed onto the American music scene in February 1964 with their historic performances in Washington D.C. and Carnegie Hall. Their music, coupled with their first class humor and personalities, firmly established them as the rock-n-roll kings for an entire generation. Their popularity, both yesterday and today, remains unequaled by any other rock-n-roll artist.

The amount of memorabilia licensed by The Beatles is vast and seemingly endless. No other group in history generated more public thirst for merchandise than The Beatles. Today's serious Beatles collectors concentrate on the early 1960s licensed Beatles items as well as the Yellow Submarine wave of memorabilia produced in 1968. North End Music Stores (NEMS) granted merchandising licenses to hundreds of companies around the world to manufacture official Beatles memorabilia. These items have become better than money in the bank as prices and demand for Beatles memorabilia continue to skyrocket. For example, a mint condition metal Beatles lunchbox in 1970 sold for $20, in 1980 $100, in 1990 $300, and as we approach the millenium, prices are upwards of $1,000.

Because The Beatles are the most collected and celebrated group in rock-n-roll history, this book is heavily weighted with hundreds of examples of prized Beatles collectibles.

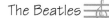

Art animation cels, 1960s, original hand-painted cels from the Beatles Saturday morning cartoon show, rare. Counterfeits exist. Set of 4, $3,000.00 – $4,000.00.

Air bed, 1964, UK, manufactured by Lilo, color variations. $700.00 – 900.00.

Apron, 1964, US, heavy reinforced paper material, repeating pattern of Beatles, stars, and records, tie straps. $400.00 – 600.00.

Assignment book, 1964, US, manufactured by Select-o-Pak, vinyl covered book has two pads of Beatles paper inside. $250.00 – 300.00.

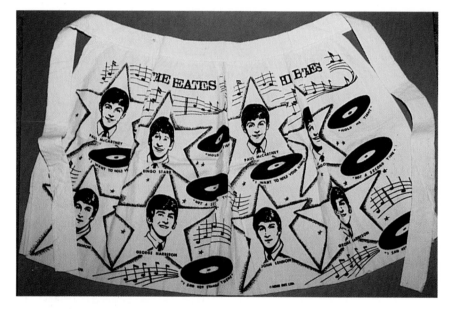

Assignment book, 1964, US, manufactured by Select-o-Pak, inside view. $250.00 – 300.00.

Autograph book, 1964, vinyl cover with blank pages inside, rare. $500.00 – 700.00. Tile, 1964, UK, manufactured by Carter, five different styles. Group picture, $250.00 – 350.00. Individual Beatle, $150.00 – 250.00 each.

Bag, 1966, Japan, vinyl bags with hangtags, additional variations. $125.00 – 150.00.

Bag, 1964, US, black vinyl with color drawings of the Beatles on both sides, rare. $1,500.00 – 2,000.00.

Balloon, 1964, US, manufactured by United Industries, various colors sealed in original packaging. $100.00 – 150.00.

Bed sheets, 1964, US, 1" piece of bed sheet each Beatle slept on during their stay at the Whittier Hotel. Counterfeits exist and lack the sailboat in the graphics. $100.00 – 150.00 set of 4.

Binders, 1964, US, colored binders manufactured by S.P.P., white binder manufactured by N. Y. L., vinyl covered three-ring notebooks. White, $150.00 – 200.00. Lavender, $350.00 – 400.00. Pink, $275.00 – 300.00. Light blue, $300.00 – 350.00. Other colors, $175.00 – 250.00.

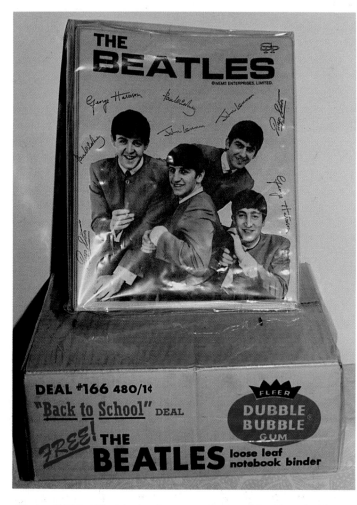

Binder, 1964, US shipping box manufactured by Fleer, held one Beatle binder. Shipping box, $400.00 – 500.00. Binder, S. P. P., $175.00 – 250.00

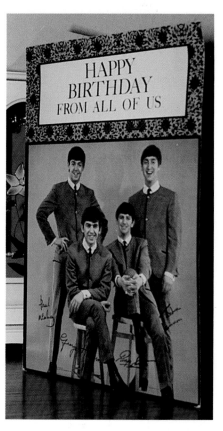

Birthday card, 1964, US, large. $35.00 – 65.00.

Books, 1960s, US & UK, various paperback and hardcover titles. Paperbacks, $15.00 – 25.00. Hardcovers, $35.00 – 75.00.

Book binder, UK, 1964, sold by the Official Beatles Fan Club to hold the Beatles Monthly magazines. Sturdy binder, gray cloth covering. $275.00 – 375.00.

Beatles Monthly book magazines, UK, 77 consecutive monthly issues, issue number 1 and 77 rarest, $100.00 – 125.00 each. Others, $20.00 – 40.00 each. Earlier issues worth more. Counterfeits exist.

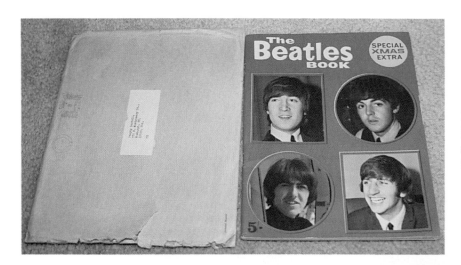

Magazine, 1965, UK, The Beatles Book Christmas Special. 1966 version not shown is priced the same. $85.00 – 100.00.

Booty bag, 1964, vinyl bag with drawstring closure and yellow paper insert. $150.00 – 175.00.

Bow, 1964, US, manufactured by Burlington, various colors and two pattern styles, attached to original display card. $300.00 – 400.00.

A brick from the original Cavern Club in Liverpool, England. $350.00 – 500.00.

Bubble bath, 1964, UK, very rare. $400.00 – 600.00.

Bubble bath containers in original boxes, 1964, manufactured by Colgate, US, only Paul and Ringo were produced. $400.00 – 500.00 each.

Bubble gum card store displays, manufactured by Topps, 1964, US. Left, first store display, red, $350.00 – 500.00. Right, second store display, new series, blue, $200.00 – 300.00. Each held 24 packs of gum cards.

Bubble gum card store displays, manufactured by Topps, 1964, US. Left, third display, color photos, series box, $200.00 – 300.00. Right, fourth display, A Hard Day's Night display, $250.00 – 350.00. Each box held 24 packs of gum cards.

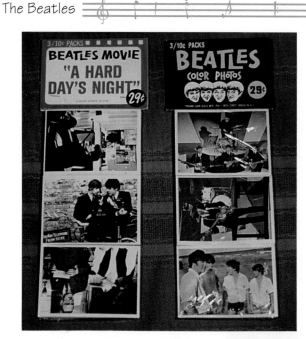

Bubble gum cards, "Rack Packs," 1964, US, manufactured by Topps, several variations. A Hard Day's Night, $200.00 – 275.00. Color photos, $200.00 – 250.00.

Bubble gum cards shipping box, 1964, US, manufactured by Topps. $600.00 – 700.00.

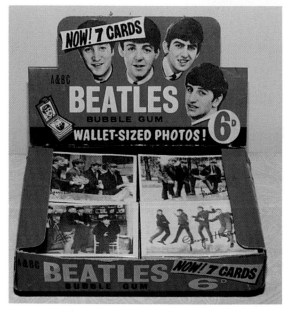

Bubble gum card store display, UK, 1964. $300.00 – 400.00.

Butcher album, 1966, US, manufactured by Capital Records, the first cover for the *Yesterday and Today* LP, several variations. First state: $3,000.00 – 8,000.00. Still pasted over, $700.00 – 1,000.00. Peeled, $700.00 – 1,000.00. Stereo copies are worth twice what mono copies are.

Buttons, 1964, US, a multitude of buttons were produced featuring the Beatles. 1" buttons, $10.00 – 12.00 each. 2" to 3½" buttons, $18.00 – 30.00 each. 7" button, I Love the Beatles, $75.00 – 100.00. Center, original advertisement for the 1" buttons, $100.00 – 200.00. Watch for reproductions!

Button, 3½", US, pinback button, rare. $50.00 – 75.00.

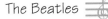

Beatles buttons promotional advertisement for Green Duck Co., 1964, US. $100.00 – 200.00. Bed sheet, 1964, US, swatch of bed linen attached to document stating the Beatles slept on this linen during their 1964 tour, various hotels. $75.00 – 100.00.

Buttons, 1964, US, set of uncut flasher buttons. $100.00 – 125.00.

Cake decorations, 1964, sealed on blister pack. $50.00 – 100.00.

Calendar, 1964, UK, "Make a date with the Beatles" easel backed plastic framed calendar, three knobs on back to change date, glass front. $450.00 – 550.00.

Calendar, 1964, UK, rare. $300.00 – 400.00.

Calendar, 1964, US, color photos of the Beatles, note calendar starts in March 1964. $125.00 – 175.00.

Cavern Club membership cards, Beatles fan club membership card. $50.00 – 75.00 each.

Christmas card, Apple Records, 1971. $75.00 – 85.00.

Christmas stocking from 1964, US, contained Beatles posters.
$50.00 – 75.00.

Christmas tree ornament, 1964, Italy, blown glass
figures with plastic brown guitars, sold in a plain
white box as a set of four (no drummer was included).
Boxed set, $800.00 – 900.00.

Chu Bops store display, miniature bubble gum
records, 1978, US. $100.00 – 200.00.

Clutch purse, manufactured in 1964 by Dame, US, 5½" x 9", various colored vinyl, zippered top with leather strap. $300.00 – 400.00. Has been reproduced. Any purse saying "NEMS Ent. Ltd. 64" is a fake. Originals are not dated.

Clutch purse, manufactured in 1964 by Dame, US, black vinyl with white printing. $350.00 – 400.00.

Colorforms, 1966, US, Colorforms toy complete with stage, body parts, and instruction book in box. $900.00 – 1,200.00.

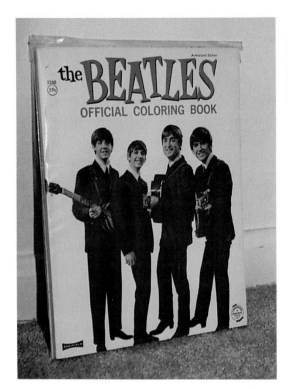

Coloring book, 1964, US, manufactured by Saalfield, unused. $75.00 – 100.00.

Comb, 1964, US, manufactured by Lido toys, various colors, 14" long with sticker attached to front. Has been reproduced. $200.00 – 300.00.

Combs, UK, on original store display, 1964. $300.00 – 400.00.

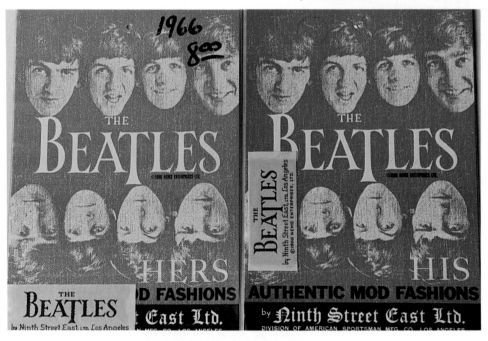

Clothing tags, 1966, US, paper tags and cloth labels for "the authentic mod fashion" line. $35.00 – 45.00.

Left to right: Coin, 1966, silver, UK with advertisement, $200.00 – 250.00. Guitar string, 1964, UK, manufactured by Hofner, sealed in package, $75.00 – 85.00. HELP! promotional band aid, 1965, US, manufactured by Capitol Records, sealed, $40.00 – 50.00. Megaphone, 1964, US, manufactured by Yellaphone, white, orange, or yellow, with chain, $700.00 – 1,000.00.

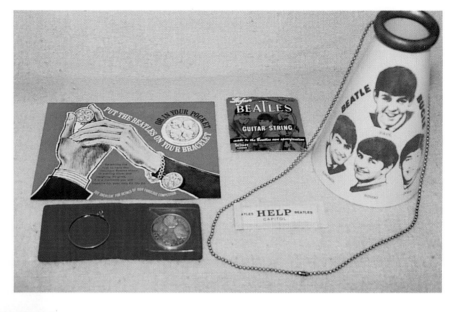

Coin holder store display, 1964, US. $700.00 – 900.00.

Colouring set, manufactured in UK by Kitfix, 1964, five different portraits and six different coloured pencils. Rare. $2,000.00 – 2,500.00.

Cup, plastic drinking cup, 1964, US, manufactured by Burritte, color photos of each Beatle on sides. Has been reproduced in a slightly different shaped cup. $75.00 – 125.00.

Cup, 1964, US, 8" tall drinking cup, by Burritte, came with green, red, or white colored liners, has been reproduced in a slightly different shape. Colors, $100.00 – 150.00. White, $75.00 – 100.00.

Curtain, 1964, Holland. Several designs and colors available. 2-panel curtains. $400.00 – 600.00.

Dartboard, 1968, UK, Apple Records, fairly rare. $2,000.00 – 3,000.00.

Dishware, pottery, 1964, UK, manufactured by Washington Pottery. Mug, $100.00 – 150.00. Plate, $80.00 – 120.00. Bowl, $125.00 – 170.00.

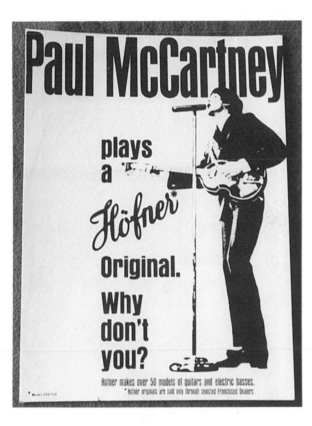

Display, store display for Hofner Instruments, 1966, US. $700.00 – 800.00.

Dolls, set of four, manufactured by Remco Industries, US, 1964, in original boxes. John & George, $300.00 – 350.00 each. Paul & Ringo, $200.00 – 250.00 each. Boxes have been counterfeited. Each box has a white cardboard inner insert to hold doll in place; counterfeit boxes usually lack this item.

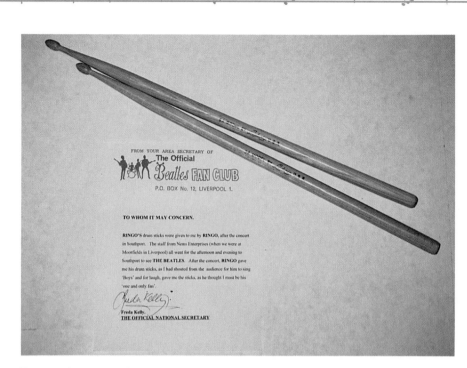

Drumsticks personally owned by Ringo Starr, given to UK fan club president Freda Kelly after the March 1963 Southport concert. $3,500.00 – 5,000.00.

Mascot doll, 1964, US, manufactured by Remco, 29" long cloth doll, available in several colors, with cardboard guitar and fold-open hangtag. $300.00 – 400.00.

Advertisement, 1964, US, by Remco displaying the mascot doll and the plastic 5" dolls. Ad, $50.00 – 75.00.

Blow-up dolls, US, 14" high inflatable vinyl dolls, one of each Beatle. Set, $175.00 – 225.00.

Dolls, The Swingers music set. 4" bobbing head dolls, sealed on display card, $100.00 – 150.00. Reproductions exist but are not sealed on backer card. Napkins, 1964, UK, package of 50 paper napkins. $450.00 – 550.00.

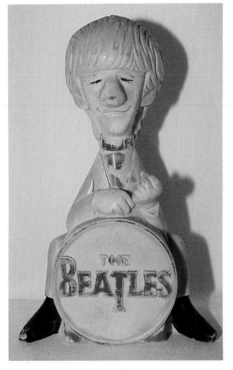

Nestlés Quik Can, has blow-up doll offer on back, chocolate and strawberry variations. $750.00 – 1,000.00. Soap box has blow-up doll offer on back, several colors, unopened. $375.00 – 475.00.

Doll, 1964, Rubber 6" figure of Ringo, manufactured by King Features. Rare. $400.00 – 600.00.

Dress, Holland, 1964, another pattern variation rarer than polka-dot pattern. Originals have a sewn-in cloth tag that says "The Beatles Dress" in red thread on a white background. $1,300.00 – 1,500.00.

Dress, 1964, manufactured in Holland, available in blue, pink, and black. $1,100.00 – 1,300.00. Reproductions exist; make sure dress is not homemade from original material.

Figurines, 1964, UK, manufactured by Sobuteo, small figures of each Beatle in original display box, $300.00 – 400.00. Book, 1964, UK & US, "In His Own Write," hardcover, first printing, $150.00 – 200.00. Second through 15th printings, $50.00 – 75.00.

Game, Flip Your Wig Game, manufactured by Milton Bradley, US, complete with board, die, cards, four playing pieces, and box inserts, 1964. $300.00 – 400.00.

Gold Record Award for "Lady Madonna" single, 1968, US, Capitol Records. Very rare. Original Gold Record Awards have white mats. These prices are for awards that were presented to the Beatles. Awards not presented to the Beatles are only worth 25% of these values. Beware of reproductions. $5,000.00 – 7,000.00.

Gold Record Award for the "Beatles '65" LP, 1965, US, Capitol Records. Originals have white mats. $6,000.00 – 8,000.00. Prices are higher depending on the L.P. for instance, a Sgt. Pepper Gold Record L.P. Award originally presented to the Beatles is valued at $15,000.00 – 20,000.00.

Drinking glasses, Dutch, 1964, set of four. $600.00 – 800.00.

Drinking glasses, left to right: Rubber coated, Ringo, black and white photo, $125.00 – 175.00. Dutch, Ringo featured, $100.00 – 125.00. Dutch, group photo, $125.00 – 175.00. George Harrison image, $125.00 – 150.00

Glasses, 1964, US, rubber coated with group picture. $175.00 – 200.00 each.

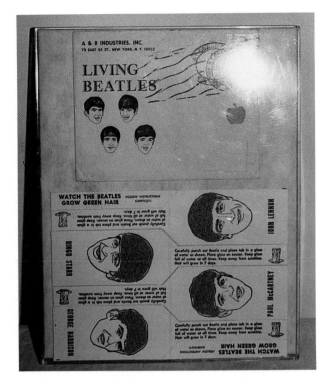

Beatle Grow Your Own Hair, 1964, US, manufactured by A & B Industries, in original mailer. Each Beatle grows "hair" when dipped into water. $500.00 – 600.00

Hair Pomade store display, Philippines, 1964, held 50 packs of pomade. Box only, $1,000.00 – 1,200.00. Single pomade pack, $75.00 – 100.00.

Left to right: Handbag, 1964, US, manufactured by Dame, white cloth with brass handle, $500.00 – 600.00. Clutch purse, 1964, US, manufactured by Dame, red vinyl with leather strap, $325.00 – 400.00. Shoulder bag, 1964, US, manufactured by Dame, various colors with rope strap, $500.00 – 600.00.

Handbag, 1964, US, manufactured by Dame, 10" x 10", various colors, with brass handles. $500.00 – 600.00.

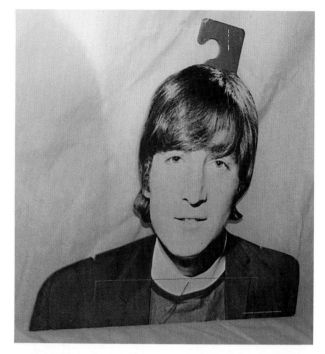

Hanger, 1964, UK, one of each Beatle. $125.00 – 150.00.

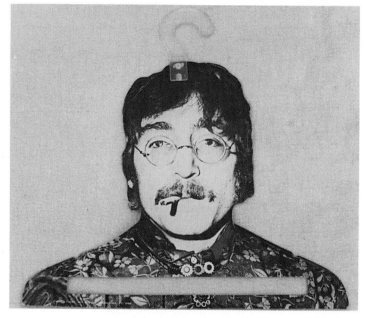

Hanger, 1968, US, clothes hanger. $150.00 – 175.00.

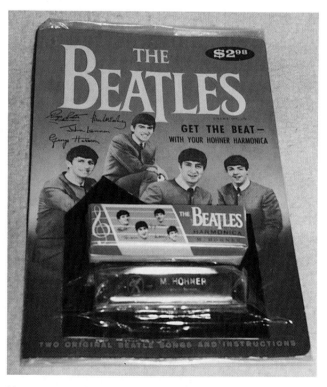

Harmonica, 1964, US, manufactured by Hohner, harmonica and box still sealed on the original cardboard fold-out display card. $500.00 – 700.00.

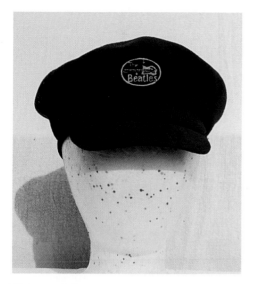

UK hat, 1964, *color variations exist (red, black, etc.).* $100.00 – 150.00.

Headphones, manufactured in 1966 by Koss Electronics, US, in original box with instructions and warranty card. $3,000.00 – 3,500.00.

Hummer, 1964, 11" long. $150.00 – 175.00.

Ice cream bar foil wrappers, US, 1964, $50.00 – 80.00 each. Bronze coin, 1964 commemorative, US, very common, $15.00 – 20.00. Ice cream bar store box, 1964, 4 or 6 bar box sizes, $500.00 – 600.00.

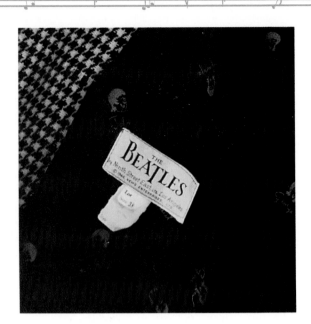

Jacket, lining displayed with original tag.

Jacket, 1960s, US, features Beatles cartoon heads with autographs on lining. $600.00 – 800.00.

Jewelry, 1964, US & UK, a myriad of Beatles officially licensed jewelry items were produced. Necklaces, $100.00 –200.00 each. Rings display card held 24 flasher rings, $1,200.00 – 1,500.00. Blue plastic ring set, $40.00 – 50.00. Metal rings and pins, $50.00 – 100.00. Bracelets, $125.00 – 225.00.

Jewelry, 1964, US, manufactured by Randall, various original necklaces, left to right: 2" wooden disk with brass figures, $250.00 – 300.00. Leather fob, $150.00 – 175.00. Pocket watch style, $100.00 – 125.00. Large leather fob, $200.00 – 250.00. Black and white group photo disk, $125.00 – 150.00. Color group drawing, $175.00 – 200.00. Fold open brass book, $150.00 – 200.00.

Jewelry, 1964, US, manufactured by Randall and Press-Initial, on original display cards. Bracelets, $100.00 – 200.00. G-clef necklace, $200.00 – 250.00. Star brooch, $250.00 – 275.00. Lariat tie, $300.00 – 400.00. Cuff links, $200.00 – 250.00. Tie clip, $125.00 – 150.00. Tie tacs, group, $100.00 – 125.00. Four tie tacs, individual, $100.00 – 125.00 set.

Jewelry, 1964, US & UK, all on original display cards. Color cuff links, $275.00 – 350.00. Beatle tac, $150.00 – 175.00. Guitar brooches, $200.00 – 250.00 set of four. Bracelet, four Beatle heads, $125.00 – 150.00. Brooch, group photo, $125.00 – 150.00. Brass guitar and 4-head tac, $35.00 – 40.00 each. Rubber vending machine figures, $75.00 – 85.00. Keychain flasher, $35.00 – 50.00. Pink Beatle brooch, $100.00 – 125.00.

Jewelry, pins store display, 1964, US, $800.00 – 1,200.00.

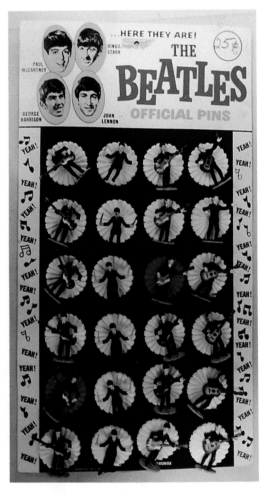

Jewelry, 1964, US, manufactured by Randall, necklace with rare variation picture of the Beatles. $250.00 – 300.00.

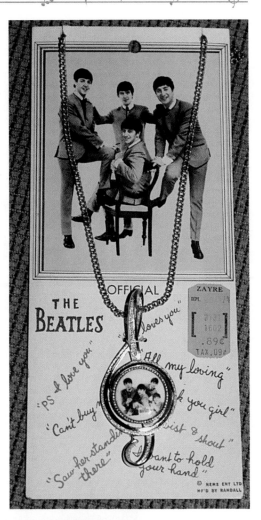

Jewelry, 1964, US, manufactured by Randall, brass G-clef with black and white photo insert of the group on 20" chain, $200.00 – 250.00.

Jewelry, 1964, US, manufactured by Randall, bracelet on the original display card. Reproductions exist, photos are slightly different. $125.00 – 150.00.

Jewelry brooch store display, 1964, US, rare. $500.00 – 600.00.

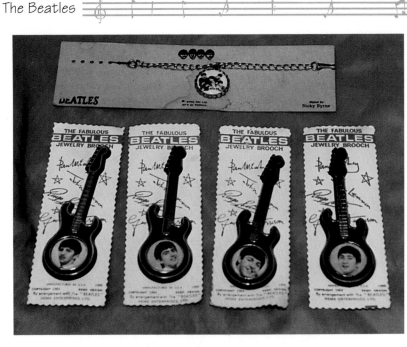

Jewelry, 1964, US, on original display cards. Reproductions exist; original cards have serrated edges, fakes are straight-edged. Bracelet, $50.00 – 75.00. Guitar brooches, $50.00 – 75.00 each.

Key ring, Apple Records. $100.00 – 150.00.

Lamp, 1964, US, floor style, 2 different pictures available, came in round or oval cylinders. $600.00 –800.00.

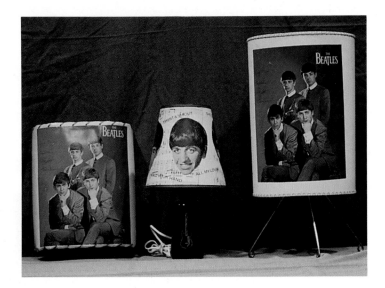

Lamps. Wall lamp, US, 2 different pictures, $400.00 – 500.00. Table lamp, UK, with original black ceramic base with gold guitar, $1,500.00 – 2,000.00. Floor lamp, round or oval cylinder with Beatles picture pasted on, 2 different pictures available, US, $600.00 – 800.00.

Lamp, 1964, UK, Beatles pictured with song titles on lampshade, wooden base. $700.00 – 1,000.00.

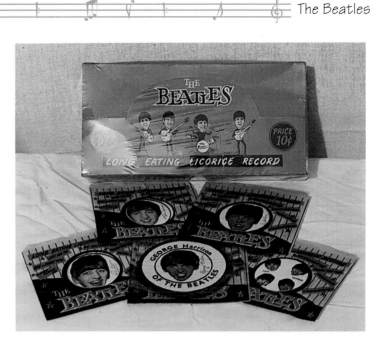

Licorice Records, 1964, UK, manufactured by Clevedon Confectionery, one of each Beatle plus a group record. Display box, $300.00 – 500.00. Records, $60.00 – 90.00 each.

Swim ring, 1965, inflatable vinyl promotional item, manufactured by United Artists for the Help! premier, 22" diameter, very rare. $4,000.00 – 6,000.00.

Loot tray, smoked glass, shallow, approximately 7" x 9", 1964. $700.00 – 1,000.00.

Magazines, 1960s, US & UK, a sampling of various magazines produced. $15.00 – 30.00.

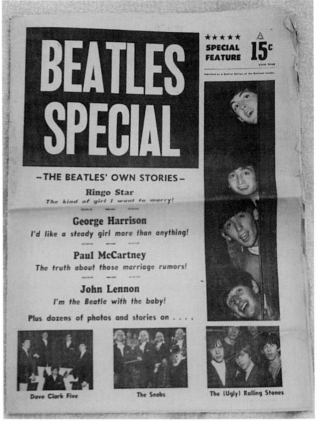

Magazine, 1964, Beatles Special newsletter. $15.00 –
20.00.

Magazines, 1964, US. Comic book, manufactured by Dell, $75.00 – 125.00. The Beatles,
$20.00 – 25.00.

Magazines, 1964, US. *The Beatles are Back*, $20.00 – 25.00. *Beatles Songs*, $15.00 – 20.00.

Magazines, 1964, US & UK. *Teen Life*, $20.00 – 25.00. *The Original Beatles Book*, $25.00 – 30.00.

Magazines, 1964, US. *Teen Life,* $20.00 – 25.00. *The Beatles Meet Dave Clark 5,* $20.00 – 25.00.

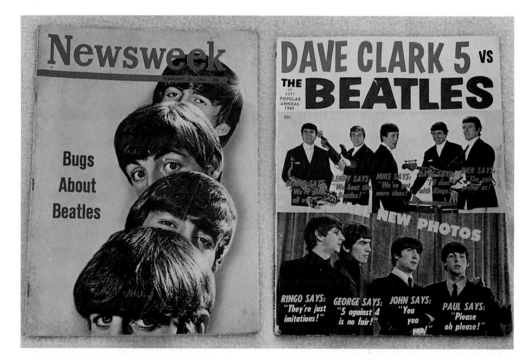

Magazines, 1964, US. *Newsweek,* $25.00 – 35.00. *Dave Clark 5 vs. the Beatles,* $20.00 – 25.00.

Magazine, 1964, UK. *Jill Meets the Beatles*, $25.00 – 30.00.

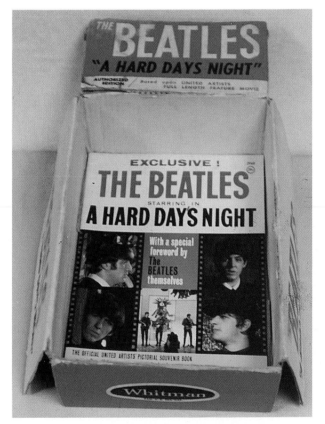

A Hard Day's Night magazine store display, 1964, US. $700.00 – 900.00. Magazine, $40.00 – 50.00.

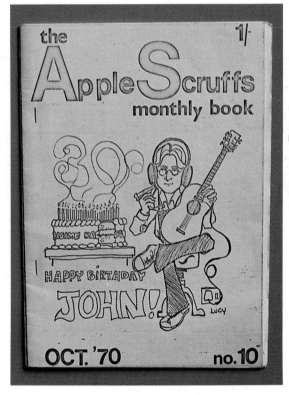

Magazine, *Apple Scruffs Monthly Book*, given to members of the Apple Scruffs. $50.00 – 60.00 each.

Money clip, Apple Records. $150.00 – 175.00.

Model kits, manufactured in UK and US by Revell, 1964, set of four, unbuilt with instructions in box. John & George, $500.00 – 600.00 each. Paul & Ringo, $300.00 – 400.00.

Movies, various black and white 8 mm short films, 1964, with original viewer and original advertisements. Price for all items, $75.00 – 100.00.

Nodders,.1964, US, manufactured by Car Mascot, 8" dolls in original box. Boxed set, $1,000.00 – 1,200.00. Reproduction nodders exist. Reproductions are numbered 1 to 4, which is impressed into the back of each Beatles' head.

Nodders, large 14" composition bobbing head dolls, manufactured by Car Mascot, 1964, set of four, promotional item only. $1,500.00 – 2,500.00 each.

Paint by number set, 1964, US, one of each Beatle, sealed in original box, manufactured by Artistic Creations. Sealed, $1,200.00 – 1,500.00. Opened, but complete, $800.00 – 1,000.00.

Patch, 1964, UK, small cloth Beatle patch. $50.00 – 75.00.

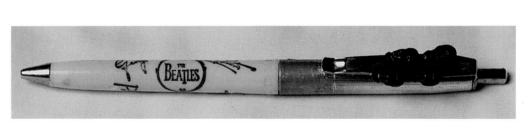

Pen, 1964, US, manufactured by Randall, close-up. $75.00 – 100.00. With original display card $125.00 – 175.00.

Left to right, top to bottom: Pencil case, black vinyl, zippered top, 4" x 7", 1964, various colors, rare, US, $300.00 – 400.00. Any pencil case marked "NEMS Ent. Ltd. 64" is a fake; originals are not marked. Wallet, manufactured in 1964 by SPP, US, various colors, complete with mirror, comb, nail file, coin holder, pictures of each Beatle, snap closure, and vinyl strap. Loose, $150.00 – 200.00 each; in original packaging, $450.00 – 700.00. Pencil case, manufactured in 1964 by SPP, US, various colored vinyl with pink being the rarest color, zippered top, 3½" x 8", loose, $150.00 – 250.00; in original cellophane package with cardboard header card, $450.00 – 700.00.

Pen holder, 1964, US, manufactured by U.S. Ceramic Co., white ceramic with color drawings of each Beatle on four ceramic disks adhered to base, with original pen and brass holder, rare. $1,000.00 – 1,300.00.

Pillow, manufactured in 1964 by Nordic House, 12" x 12", blue or red back, with original tags, four styles, US. Headshots, $175.00 – 200.00. Half bodies, $200.00 – 250.00. Full bodies, $300.00 – 400.00. Headshots with carrying strap $300.00 – 400.00.

Poster, 1964, foreign, "A Hard Day's Night" movie poster, one sheet size, rare. $400.00 – 500.00.

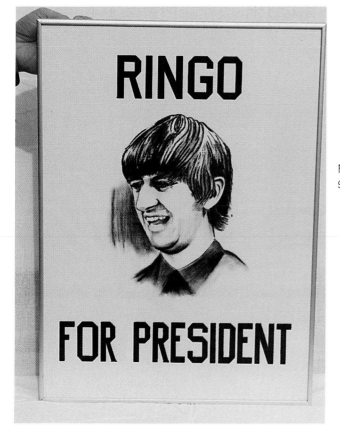

Poster, 1964, US, Ringo for President. $150.00 – 200.00.

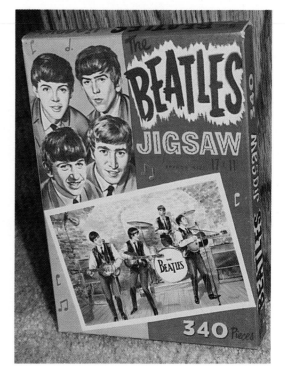

Puzzle, jigsaw, 1964, UK, 340 pieces, four different puzzles, values are for sealed puzzles only. $450.00 – 550.00 each.

Puzzle, jigsaw, 1964, UK, second version, sealed value, $450.00 – 550.00. Opened but complete, $150.00 – 250.00.

Puzzle, jigsaw, 1964, UK, third version, sealed value, $450.00 – 550.00.

Puzzle, jigsaw, 1964, UK, fourth version, sealed value, $450.00 – 550.00.

Puzzle, 1970, UK, The Beatles Illustrated Lyrics jigsaw puzzle, includes poster and puzzle solutions, 800+ pieces, complete in original box. $200.00 – 300.00.

Record carrying case, 1964, UK, manufactured by Seagull, Beatles photo under vinyl, held 45 records, plastic handles and plastic sleeves inside, various photos used. $175.00 – 250.00.

Record carrying case, 1964, US, manufactured by Air Flite, held 45 records, available in red or green colors. $500.00 – 700.00. L.P. version also made, $600.00 – 800.00.

Record carrying cases, Disk-Go-Cases, held 45 records, various colors, 1966, manufactured by Charter Industries, US. Brown is the rarest color, $500.00 – 600.00. Other colors, $250.00 – 350.00. Original hang tag, $150.00 – 200.00. Wraparound Beatle banner, $150.00 – 200.00. Cardboard insert, $40.00 – 50.00.

Disk-Go-Case store display banner, 1964, US, manufactured by Charter Industries. $700.00 – 1,000.00.

Record player, 1964, electric, US, 4-speed turntable, 17" x 10" and 6", has Beatles pictured inside and outside on top right, in working condition. $6,000.00 – 8,000.00.

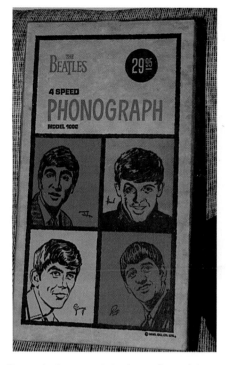

Record player, original cardboard box, complete with instructions, the box is extremely rare, 1964, US. $6,000.00 – 8,000.00.

Ringo Roll, 1964, UK, bread package, rare. $400.00 – 600.00.

Record set, Italian, Apple, with interview disk, open view. $600.00 – 700.00.

Record set, Italian, Apple, with interview disk, closed view.

Rug, 1964, Belgium, colorful woven rug, original tag on back does not say Beatles. $350.00 – 450.00.

School bag, 1964, manufactured in Canada, with original handle and strap, $2,500.00 – 3,000.00. Compact, 1964, UK, brass with black and white photo of the Beatles on top, inside had mirror, makeup, and puff. Loose, $300.00 – 400.00. Boxed, $500.00 – 600.00.

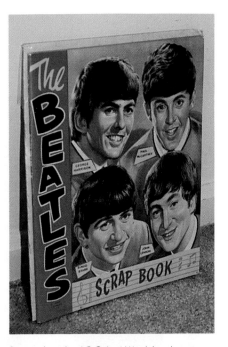

Scrapbook, 1964, UK, blank pages inside, $75.00 – 85.00. US version, same pricing.

Shampoo shipping box/store display, 1964, US, manufactured by Bronson, Held bottles of shampoo, which have yet to be found. $700.00 – 1,000.00.

Sheet music, 1960s, US. Many of their songs were available. $20.00 – 25.00 each.

Shoulder bag, UK, 1964, black canvas with faces on front, autographs on back, very rare. $2,000.00 – 3,000.00.

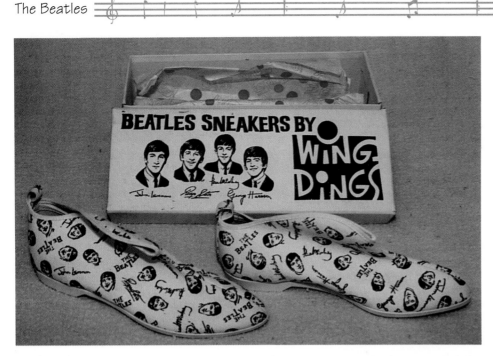

Pink sneakers are rarely found.

Sneakers, 1964, US, manufactured by Wing Dings, several colors and two styles. White low tops, boxed, $1,000.00 – 1,200.00. White high tops, boxed, $1,200.00 – 1,500.00. Blue low tops, boxed, $1,100.00 – 1,300.00. Blue high tops, boxed, $1,400.00 – 1,800.00. Pink low tops boxed, manufactured in Canada, $2,000.00 – 2,500.00.

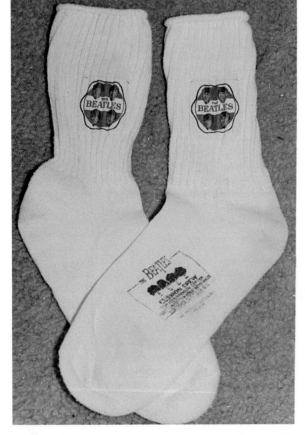

Beatle stamps, two different varieties, 1964, US. Hallmark booklet of 100 stamps, $35.00 – 45.00. Sheet of black and white stamps, $40.00 – 50.00.

Socks, 1964, US, pair of Beatle socks with ironed-on emblems. Rare. Loose, $400.00 – 600.00. In original packaging with B/W photo card, $800.00 – 1,200.00.

Sunglasses store display, cardboard, 1964, US, manufactured by Bachman Bros. Display, $800.00 – 1,000.00. Sunglasses, $200.00 – 250.00 each.

Tickets to "A Hard Day's Night" and "Help!" movie premiers, 1964 – 1965, US. Tickets, $50.00 – 60.00 each. Badge, $25.00 – 30.00.

Talc tin, UK, 1964, manufactured by Margo of Mayfair, 7" high, photographs of Beatles on front and back, $600.00 – 1,000.00. Perfume, UK, 1964, manufactured by Olive Adair of Liverpool, very rare, brown paper label, $3,000.00 – 5,000.00. Hairspray, US, 1964, manufactured by Bronson, 8" high can with paper label, normally seen with pink label but other pastel colors exist. Reproductions exist. Bottom of can on originals has been machine stamped with an 'SD' I.D. number. $1,000.00 – 1,500.00.

Hair spray, UK, exact vintage unknown. $1,000.00 – 1,500.00.

Tape, 1964, Philippines, manufactured by Starlight Commercial, cardboard store display held 12 packages of Beatle Tape. Display, $1,000.00 – 1,200.00. One tape, $300.00 – 400.00.

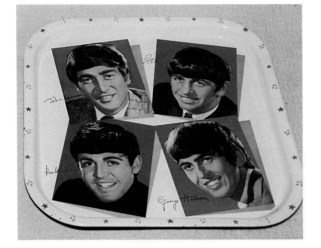

Tray, metal tea tray, 1964, UK, original says "Made in Gt. Britain" on front. Fakes exist; fakes say "Made in England." Some originals have a paper manufacturer's label on the back. $75.00 – 100.00.

Tray, 1964, Japan, large or small bamboo serving tray, 6" to 11". Three sizes exist. $100.00 – 150.00.

Apple Wristwatch, 1968, UK, Apple Records promotional piece, with original band. Loose, $700.00 – 800.00. Boxed $1,200.00 – 1,400.00.

Vinyl material, 1964, UK. This vinyl could be purchased in various sizes, 2' x 4' panel., $400.00 – 500.00.

Wallet photos booklet store display, 1964, US. store display, $350.00 – 450.00. Wallet photo booklet, $25.00 – 35.00.

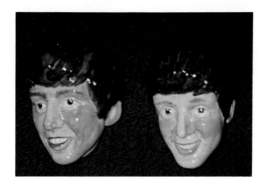

Wall plaques, 1964, UK, manufactured by Kelsboro Ware, 5" ceramic handpainted heads of each Beatle. Watch for reproductions. Originals have a company ink stamp on back. $400.00 – 500.00 each.

Watch, 1964, UK, manufactured by Smiths, in original box with outer sleeve. Value for complete item. There were only three watches that were originally produced in the 1960s: this one, the Apple wristwatch manufactured by Old England UK 1968, and Sheffield Yellow Submarine wristwatch. $1,400.00 – 2,000.00.

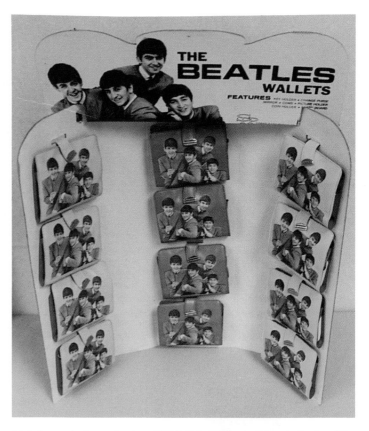

Wallets and store display, 1964, US, SPP, cardboard display. Display only, $2,000.00 – 2,500.00. Wallets, $150.00 – 200.00 each.

Wig, US, 1964, manufactured by Lowell Toys, sealed with original header card. Value for sealed item only. Reproductions exist. $125.00 – 150.00.

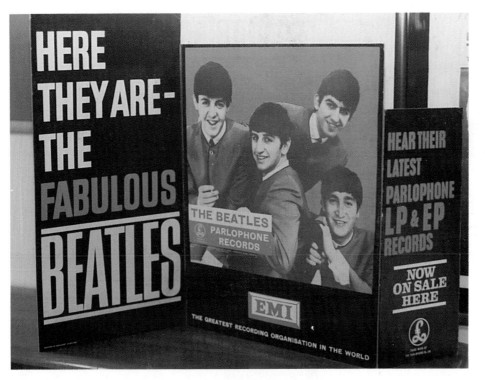

Beatles early countertop promotional display from the UK, 1963, rare. $4,000.00 – 6,000.00

Beatles, "Meet the Beatles" large cardboard. electric store display, 1964, US, Capitol Records, rare. $10,000.00 – 15,000.00.

Beatles, "Something New" promotional poster, 1964, Capitol Records. $1,500.00 – 2,000.00.

"Beatles VI" L.P. promotional cardboard display, 1965, US, Capitol Records. $3,000.00 – 4,000.00.

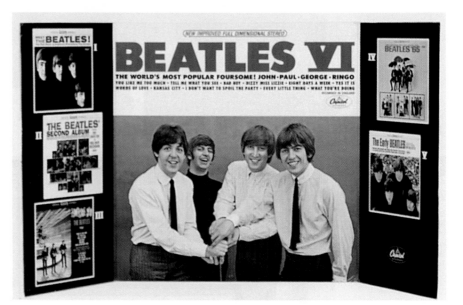

Beatles "Help!" L.P. promotional poster, 1965, US, Capitol Records. $1,000.00 – 1,500.00.

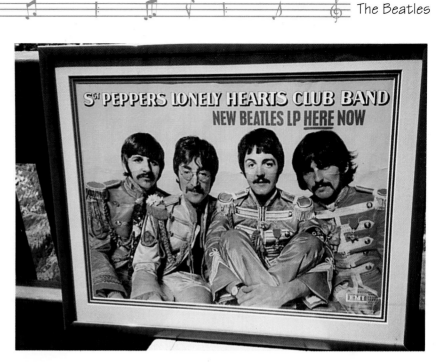

Beatles "Rubber Soul" L.P. promotional poster, 1965, US, Capitol Records. $600.00 – 800.00.

Beatles "Sergeant Pepper's Lonely Hearts Club" L.P. promotional poster, 1967, UK, EMI Records. $1,000.00 – 1,500.00.

Beatles "Help!" electric store display, 1965, US, Capitol Records. $5,000.00 – 7,000.00.

Beatles "Magical Mystery Tour" L.P. promotional poster, 1967, US, Capitol Records. $1,000.00 – 1,500.00.

Beatles "White Album" promotional poster, UK, 1968, EMI Records. $800.00 – 1,000.00.

Yellow Submarine, 2' circular cardboard display, diecut around top, 1968, US, very rare. $2,000.00 – 2,500.00.

Beatles "Yellow Submarine" promotional poster, either rolled or folded and inserted with *Billboard* magazine, 1968, US. Rolled, $600.00 – 800.00. Folded, $400.00 – 600.00.

"Yellow Submarine" promotional mobile display, 1968, Italy. $700.00 – 800.00.

Beatles "Abbey Road" L.P. promotional cardboard display, 5' high record bin, 1969, US, Capitol Records. $3,000.00 – 5,000.00.

"Yellow Submarine" motorized promotional L.P. cardboard display. 5' high. Submarine rotates, powered by a battery-operated motor. Very rare, 1868, US, Capitol Records. $7,500.00 – 10,000.00.

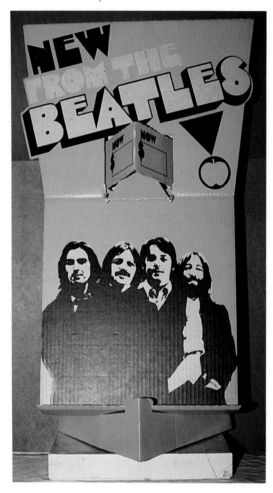

Beatles "Let It Be" L.P. promotional poster, 1970, US, Capitol Records. $750.00 – 900.00.

Beatles "Hey Jude" L.P. countertop promotional display, 1970, US, Capitol Records. $1,600.00 – 1,700.00.

Beatles "Something/Come Together" promotional poster, 1969, US, Capitol Records. $600.00 – 700.00.

Beatles 1962 – 1970 45 countertop promotional display, 1970, US, Capitol Records. $400.00 – 500.00.

Elvis Presley

There can be no doubt in anyone's mind that without Elvis Presley, rock-n-roll wouldn't have been the same, or for all practical purposes may not have been at all. Elvis's efforts molded, inspired, and developed rock-n-roll through the generations to what it is today. Unlike any before him, Elvis had a raw and unseen talent, a talent that will quite likely never be matched again in rock history. Elvis's success in the music and film industries won him the title "The King of Rock-n-Roll." For many, Elvis is the most popular recording artist in the history of rock music.

When we think of Elvis, it's hard to believe he was ever anything but successful. However, in his earlier years he once drove a delivery truck for $35 a week. After several unsuccessful songs on the Sun label, Elvis's contract was sold to RCA in 1955 for an unheard of $35,000. His popularity quickly skyrocketed with his first hit, "Heartbreak Hotel," that spent eight weeks at number one in 1956. Through his career Elvis charted an unbelievable 107 Top 40 hits, more than twice that of The Beatles. He also had the most Top 10 recordings and has spent more weeks in the number one position (80 weeks) than anyone else.

With his success in the 1950s came the immediate need for merchandise. Elvis Presley Enterprises created a huge wave of memorabilia for hungry Elvis fans. The merchandise created by Elvis Presley Enterprises in 1956 is the most valuable and sought after of all the memorabilia marketed. Merchandise that appeared his death in 1977 is of value as well, due to his unaging interest.

Elvis, like Marilyn Monroe, Jim Morrison, and other famous personalities, has had continuing success long after his death, possibly more than anyone in modern history. Elvis memorabilia was fueled by his death and continues to be manufactured today.

However, the pre-1970s merchandise continues to hold the most collectible and monetary value. The availability of most Elvis items is scarce. Especially hard to find are those items of the 1950s that have become extremely rare and continue to demand the highest of values at auctions and sales. Elvis memorabilia will always be of collectible value and is always worthy of investment.

"King Galahad" punching bag balloon, $60.00 – 100.00. "Jailhouse Rock" flipbook, $50.00 – 75.00. "Tickle Me" feather pen, $30.00 – 40.00.

Buttons, left to right: 1956, 3" cardboard back, $100.00 – 110.00. Early Elvis Fan Club, $150.00 – 160.00. I Love Elvis, $35.00 – 40.00. I Hate Elvis, $35.00 – 40.00.

Bronzed bookend, 1956, E.P.E. $350.00 – 375.00.

Flasher pins, left to right: 3" red rim, vari-vue, 1956, $25.00. 3" blue rim, vari-vue, 1956, $25.00. B/W with plastic frame, $40.00. Keychain, 1956, $20.00. Original E.P.E. Pictorial Productions Inc., 1956, $35.00. Color flasher, 1956, $25.00. B/W flasher, 1956, $20.00.

Pinback buttons, late 1950s, 7/8". Top row: "Blue Suede Shoes," "Blue Suede Shoes," "Love Me Tender." Bottom row: "Anyway You Want Me," "Hound Dog," "I Want You, I Need You, I Love You." $50.00 each.

Pinback buttons, 7/8". Gum machine items, set of six. Each $30.00 – 35.00. Far right button, rare, E.P.E., 1956. $90.00 – 100.00.

Overnight case, 1956, by E.P.E. $600.00 – 750.00.

Clocks, left to right: Unknown manufacturer, $40.00 – 50.00. 1987, E.P.E., $40.00 – 50.00.) 1977, "Love Me Tender," Unique Time Co., $70.00 – 90.00. Bradley E.P.E., $35.00 – 45.00.

Coaster, 3½", E.P.E., 1956. $340.00 – 360.00.

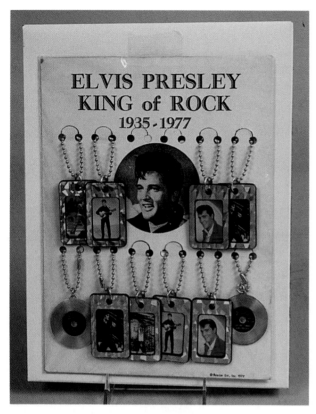

Keychain display, Boxcar, 1977. $125.00 – 135.00.

Picture disc display, $85.00 – 95.00. Chu Bops bubble gum display, complete, $85.00 – 95.00.

Dolls, left to right: All Elvis Presley Enterprises. Eugene, 1984, $85.00 – 95.00. Hasbro, 1993, $20.00 – 40.00. World, 1984, $210.00 – 250.00.

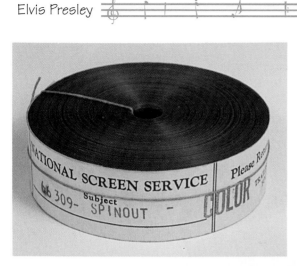

"Spinout" film trailer. Shown in theatres as coming attractions and returned when feature film was received. Undetermined value.

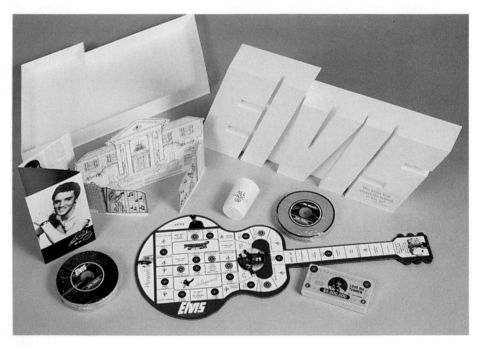

Game, "Elvis – The Game That Allows The Legend To Live On!", 1987, E.P.E., S. Alden Inc. $50.00 – 75.00.

"Love Me Tender" hair and body care products display, $45.00 – 55.00. Bottle of rinse, $35.00 – 45.00.

"G.I. Blues" paper hat movie promotion, $100.00 – 150.00. Army belt, West Germany, 1960s, rare, undetermined value.

Crew hat with tag, 1956, E.P.E., $120.00 – 140.00. T-shirt, 1956, E.P.E., $440.00 – 460.00.

Jewelry: E.P.E., 1956, US. "Loving You" charm bracelet, $50.00 – 75.00. "Loving You" earrings, $75.00 – 100.00. Pierced earrings, $200.00 – 225.00.

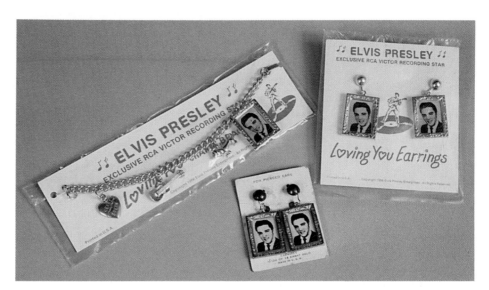

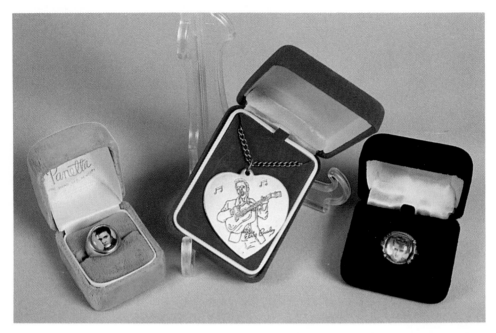

Jewelry, adjustable rings. Left: re-issue of original, $50.00 – 75.00. Far right, 1956 issue, $160.00 – 175.00. Heart necklace, $180.00 – 200.00. Signed on back. "Sincerely Yours," Elvis Presley, 1956, E.P.E.

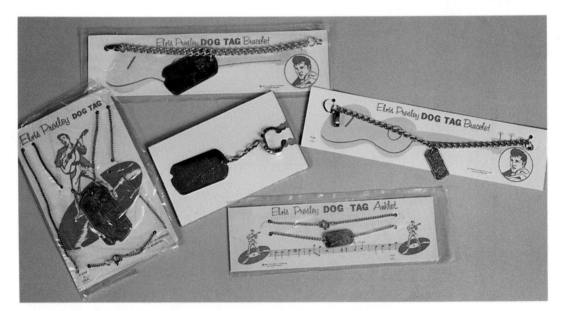

Dog tag jewelry. Necklace, $70.00 – 80.00. Bracelet (men's), $30.00 – 40.00. Keychain, $75.00 – 100.00. Bracelet (lady's), $30.00 – 40.00. Anklet, $40.00 – 50.00.

Lei and medallion, $190.00 – 225.00. "Blue Hawaii" postcard, 6" x 9", $70.00 – 75.00.

Lobby cards. "Jailhouse Rock," $800.00 – 850.00 per set. "Blue Hawaii," $350.00 – 400.00 per set.

Magazines, 1950s, left to right: Elvis Presley, "The Intimate Story," $110.00 – 125.00. "Official Elvis Presley Album Life Story," $90.00 – 110.00. "The Amazing Elvis Presley," $100.00 – 120.00. "Elvis Presley Speaks," $90.00 – 110.00.

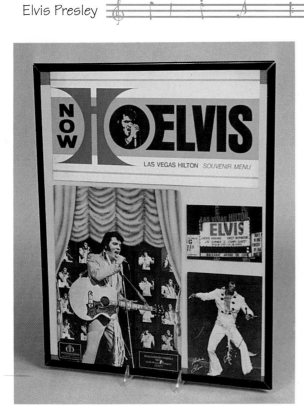

Las Vegas menu. "Elvis Now," Hilton, $35.00 – 40.00. International Hotel, 1971, $45.00 – 50.00. Vegas postcard, $25.00 – 30.00.

Las Vegas menus, Hilton. Jan. 26 – Feb. 9, 1974, $35.00 – 45.00. Jan. 26 – Feb. 23, 1972, $45.00 – 55.00.

Pencil set, 12-pack by E.P.E., 1956, $250.00 – 300.00.

Pennants, left to right: "King of Rock & Roll," $20.00 – 30.00. "The one and Only," $40.00 – 50.00. Birthplace Tupelo, Miss., E.P.E., 1962, $40.00 – 50.00.

Assorted perfumes, left to right: "Teddy Bear" perfume (1957 but probably was later), $75.00 – 125.00. Elvis cologne, 1990s, $20.00 – 30.00. "Teddy Bear" perfume with box by E.P.E., 1956, $250.00 – 300.00.

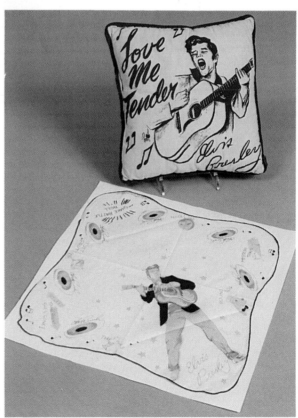

Pillow, "Love Me Tender," 1956, E.P.E., $370.00 – 400.00. Scarf, handkerchief, 1956, $475.00 – 500.00.

Photos, left to right: 1956 publicity photo with plastic frame, unknown manufacturer, $75.00 – 100.00. Fan club photos, 1956, wallet, $15.00 – 20.00; 5" x 7", $30.00 – 35.00.

Jigsaw puzzles, Elvisly Yours, London, England. $25.00 – 40.00 each.

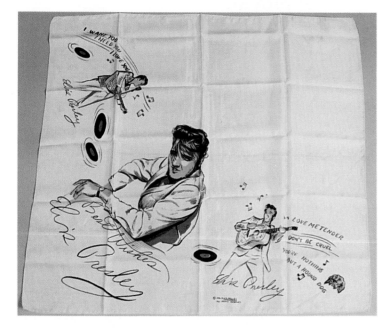

Head scarf, 1956, E.P.E. $550.00 – 575.00.

Sheet music, left to right: "Hound Dog," $45.00 – 55.00. "It's Now or Never," $30.00 – 40.00. "Love Me," $30.00 – 40.00. "One Night," $35.00 – 45.00.

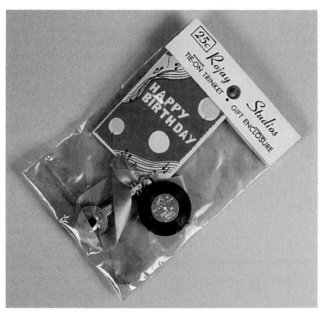

Package tie-on and gift enclosure, 1950s. Record shows RCA Victor with dog, titled "Don't Be Cruel" with "Sing Elvis Sing" on the reverse side, small guitar attached. $75.00 – 100.00.

Gold Record Award for the L.P. "Elvis – A Legendary Performer, Vol. I," US, RCA Records. $10,000.00 – 12,000.00.

KISS

It's hard to believe a band with no television exposure and only one fluke Top 10 hit could attract so much attention. Somehow the masked members of the rock band KISS did. It was obviously only a matter of time and the evolving transition of glitzy glamour rock of the early 1970s before someone would cover their entire face in makeup for added attention. Gene Simmons, Paul Stanley, Ace Frehley, and Peter Criss took glamour rock one step farther for unprecedented success. They wore outrageous costumes, presented unbelievable stage shows, and wowed their fans who couldn't, or wouldn't, relate to the co-existing disco movement.

KISS music, except for their only Top 10 hit "Beth," brought back the danger element of rock music. Along with this was the mystery of who they really were – but today we know! Although KISS never made it in the pop market, the group won millions of fans in the rock-n-roll arena. From their growing popularity in 1975 came the creation of the KISS Army, the group's fan club, which was just the beginning of what was to perpetuate one of the largest memorabilia merchandising floods of all time.

Up to this point only The Beatles and Elvis Presley had enjoyed success of this caliber from the sale of toys and memorabilia. Both of these acts had a huge listenership on AM radio and lots of exposure on television. The merchandising success of KISS baffled the critics. For the very first time a rock, as opposed to pop, band could support itself.

KISS memorabilia is extremely collectible and somewhat scarce. The question is, with so many items produced in the not too distant 1970s, where did it all go? Original KISS items from the 1970s are becoming as hard to find as Elvis items from the 1950s and Beatles items of the 1960s. The scarcity of 1970s KISS memorabilia will only increase its collective and investment potential in the rock-n-roll music market place.

Assorted belt buckles, 1976 – 1979. With face picture, $75.00 – 100.00. With Kiss logo, $50.00 – 75.00. All others, $30.00 – 50.00.

Series 1 or 2 gum card boxes, full, $100.00 – 150.00. Series 1 card case, $100.00 – 125.00. Rock stars card box, $15.00 – 25.00.

Pinback buttons. Large, $15.00 – 20.00. Small, $10.00 – 12.00. Kiss Army, $20.00 – 25.00. Unlicensed buttons, $3.00 – 5.00.

Majick Market cups, 1978. Each $75.00 –100.00. Center: Pepsi screamer, sold at concerts with beverage, bottom of cup could then be pushed out to become a screaming instrument, $50.00 – 75.00. Note: Blue version of screamer (not pictured), considered rare. $100.00 – 150.00.

Dolls boxed, $200.00 – 250.00. Dolls loose, $125.00 – 175.00.

"The Kiss Army" fan club kits, $50.00 – 85.00.

"On Tour" board game by Aucoin, 1978, $150.00 – 175.00. Colorforms by Colorforms, 1979, $75.00 – 125.00. Rub 'n Play by Colorforms, 1979, $125.00 – 200.00.

Gold Record Album for "Rock & Roll Over" album. $500.00 – 550.00.

Selection of jewelry, Aucoin, 1977. $30.00 – 50.00 each.

Black flame tour jacket (back shown). $150.00 – 200.00.

Tour jacket. $75.00 – 100.00.

Keychains, one made of each member, Aucoin, 1977. $50.00 – 75.00 each.

Halloween costumes, 1978, boxed. $150.00 – 200.00 each.

Lunchbox, by Thermos, 1979, $150.00 – 200.00. Thermos for lunchbox, $25.00 – 45.00. Backpack by Thermos, 1979, $200.00 – 250.00. Puffy stickers (set of four), by Rocksticks, 1979, $150.00 – 200.00. Logo shoelaces, unknown manufacturer, 1979, $40.00 – 60.00. Kids belt, unknown manufacturer, 1978, $100.00 – 150.00.

Make-up kits, two versions, by Remco, 1978. $200.00 – 250.00.

Mirrors, 1977 – 1979, $50.00 – 60.00 each.

Spiral notebooks, $30.00 – 45.00 each. School folder, $40.00 – 50.00.

Ballpoint pens, 1978, on card, $100.00 – 125.00 each. Pencil set, 1978, sealed on card, $75.00 – 100.00.

Press kits, make-up era, $50.00 – 150.00. The Elder, rare, $200.00 – 250.00.

Jigsaw puzzles, Milton Bradley, 1977 – 1978, $65.00 – 125.00 each.

Transistor radio, by Kiss/Aucoin, 1977. $150.00 – 200.00; with box, $200.00 – 250.00. (Note original store price on box of $9.95!)

Rockdoms, $5.00 – 8.00. Keychain, $10.00 – 15.00. Mardi Gras coins, $25.00 – 30.00 each. Matchbook covers, $5.00 – 8.00.

Sheet music. $10.00 – 20.00 each.

Songbooks: "The Originals," $100.00 – 150.00. "Unmasked," $100.00 – 150.00. Both rare.

Trash can, Aucoin, 1977. $175.00 – 250.00.

Radio control van with transmitter, 1979, $500.00 – 575.00. Custom Chevy van model kit, AMT, 1977, $150.00 – 200.00.

Optical reels shown with viewers. View-Master reel set with envelope, GAF, 1978, $50.00 – 75.00. Double-Vue on card GAF, 1978, $200.00 – 250.00. Show Beam cartridge in package, GAF, 1978, $200.00 – 250.00.

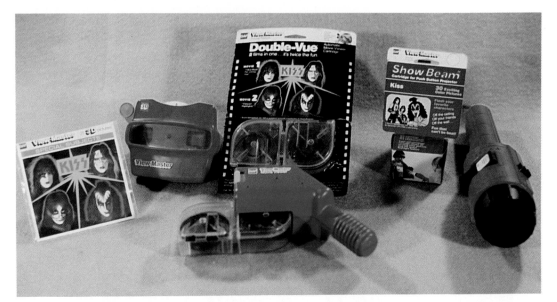

Pocket watch, unlicensed item. $40.00 – 60.00.

The Monkees

After more than 400 people were interviewed, America's answer to The Beatles was born. These whimsical, nutty mop-tops became an overnight sensation when their television show aired on NBC-TV September 12, 1966. Of the four, Mike Nesmith and Peter Tork had some musical experience. Micky Dolenz had acting experience (Circus Boy) and Davy Jones was a jockey in England who also sang in "Oliver!"

Producers Bert Schneider and Bob Rafelson created The Monkees show while Don Kirshner (with some help from his already successful songwriting friends) created massive hits for them to record. The zany, quick-moving, prime-time TV show was based on the same format as The Beatles "A Hard Day's Night" and "Help!". Their slapstick humor and two songs per show brought both The Monkees and their music instant stardom. The show ran for 58 episodes until its ratings were hurt by "Gunsmoke" and dropped in 1968.

The Monkees had a total of 11 Top 40 hits, six of which went gold. But studio session musicians played the music and with the exception of some vocals, the recordings were not done by the Monkees at all. After gaining confidence and popularity, The Monkees severed their relationship with Kirshner, recorded a bit on their own, and eventually broke up in 1970. Kirshner tried again and hit it big with The Archies, a cartoon band. Several attempts at regrouping The Monkees were tried with only marginal success but with a minor hit "That Was Then, This Is Now" in 1986. The Monkees also played an important role as a stepping stone for the development of very successful MTV (Music Television).

An abundance of items was created for The Monkees. With few exceptions, all Monkees memorabilia is of value. Appearing less frequently through the years, these items have demanded top dollar. Monkees items today are appreciating nearly as fast as Beatles and Kiss items.

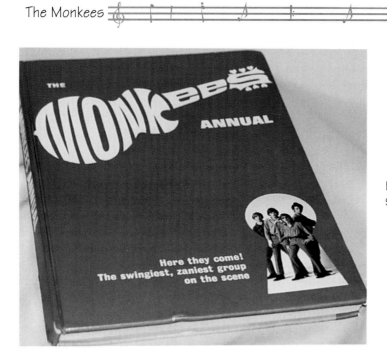

Book, 1967, Raybert Productions, U.K., 1967 Annual. $35.00 – 60.00.

Book, 1968, Century 21 Publishing, U.K., 1968 Annual. $35.00 – 60.00.

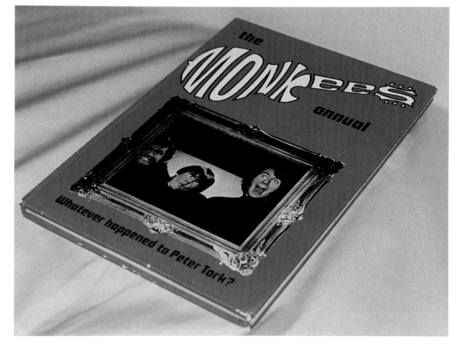

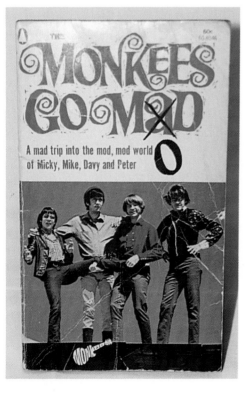

Book, 1967, Raybert Productions, The Monkees "Go Mad/Mod." $15.00 – 20.00.

Charm bracelet, 1967, Raybert, Loose, $35.00 – 50.00; carded, $75.00 – 100.00.

Bubble gum cards, 1966 – 1967, Don Russ, US. $1.00 – 2.00 each.

Records, Colgems, Post Cereal, 1967 – 1968, record cut-outs. $20.00 – 35.00 each.

Monkees buttons, 1966, Raybert. Set of four, $35.00.

True fan button, 1966, Raybert. $15.00 – 20.00.

Pins, 1", Raybert, 1967, US. Mint, $10.00 each or $50.00 set of 5.

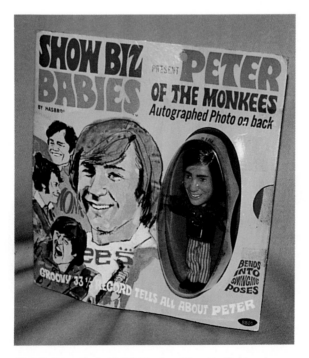

Keychain, 1966, Raybert. $15.00 – 25.00.

4" doll, Peter Tork, 1967, Hasbro Showbiz Babies. Loose, $75.00 – 100.00; carded, $200.00 – 250.00.

Game, 1967, Raybert Productions, Transogram, "The Monkees" Game, US. Opened but complete, $75.00 – 125.00; sealed, $200.00 – 250.00.

6" Corgi Monkeemobile, various colors and versions made. 1967 – 1968. $200.00 – 300.00.

Pen, 1967, Raybert. $25.00 – 30.00.

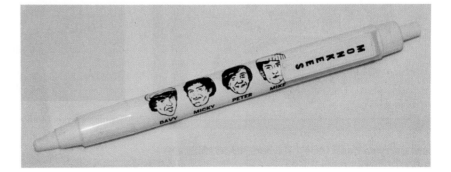

"Body of Evidence" promo passion pack kit included candle, candle holder, handcuffs, shipping box, bubble bath in bottle (plastic), champagne glass (plastic). Rare promo item. Few issued through fan club. $175.00 – 250.00.

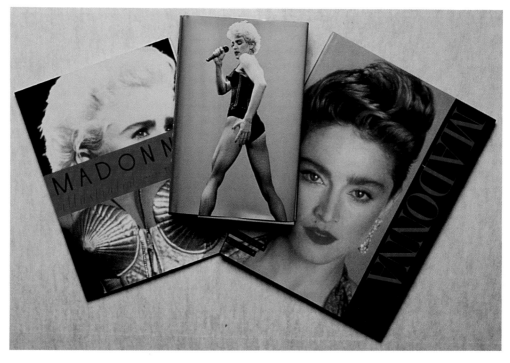

Assorted books, 1990s. $20.00 – 25.00.

Game, 1967, Raybert Productions, Transogram, "The Monkees" Game, US. Opened but complete, $75.00 – 125.00; sealed, $200.00 – 250.00.

6" Corgi Monkeemobile, various colors and versions made. 1967 – 1968. $200.00 – 300.00.

Pen, 1967, Raybert. $25.00 – 30.00.

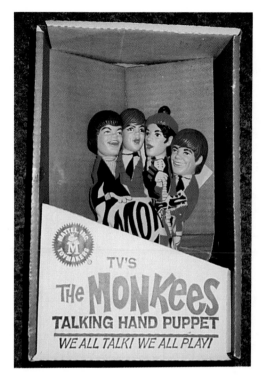

Talking hand puppet, sealed in original box, Mattel, 1968. $150.00 – 225.00.

Jigsaw puzzle, Fairchild, four different designs, 1967, Raybert Productions. $75.00 – 100.00.

Record carrying case (45s), Raybert, 1966. $125.00 – 200.00.

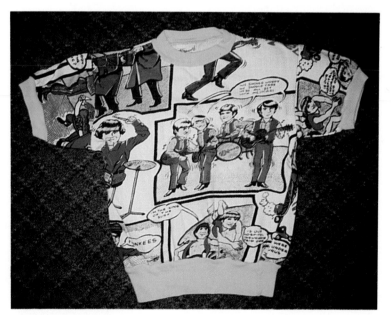

T-shirt (note Monkees logo on tag), 1967 – 1968, Monkees fashions with logo label are rare. Raybert, US. $300.00 – 400.00.

Madonna

It seems with Madonna you have two choices: either you love her or you hate her. Whichever you choose, you cannot deny her popularity and success. In addition to being number one in more countries than any other singer, Madonna has also become the most successful singer on record. Madonna's strong musical and acting careers together with her views on sexuality have made her a household name. Her unrelenting desire to succeed and being at the right place at the right time have kept Madonna always ahead of the game. One only guesses what she'll do next.

Madonna did to fashion in the 1980s what Sonny and Cher did 20 years earlier. With her success came the age of the Madonna look-alike. But Madonna always goes further and creates so many new looks that it's hard to keep up with her latest styles.

While Madonna's pro-disco music was climbing the charts to make her a star, *Penthouse* and *Playboy* magazines published some nude photos taken of her years before. The successful sales of these magazines prompted a new age of Madonna, one of pushing the limits in sexuality and a lack, some think, of moral guidelines to unseen heights. Madonna's success on the screen has also made her a credible actress. But it's really her character that leaves people guessing.

Madonna's book entitled *Sex* was released in 1992 to a not-so-shy audience. The book proved once again that Madonna could push the limits, achieve new heights, and, as usual, be slightly ahead of the game.

It is likely that Madonna's memorabilia will become of collectible value. Many items have been merchandised by Boy Toy Inc., Madonna's Company, and distributed through her fan club. Though many items are currently available through the fan club, not many have made their way into the collector circuit. Breathless Mahoney items, from the character she played in the film "Dick Tracy," disappeared rapidly from circulation in the relatively short time they were available. The 18" Breathless doll doubled in value in just a few months after its debut. This is a good indication of what the market may hold for Madonna memorabilia.

"Body of Evidence" promo passion pack kit included candle, candle holder, handcuffs, shipping box, bubble bath in bottle (plastic), champagne glass (plastic). Rare promo item. Few issued through fan club. $175.00 – 250.00.

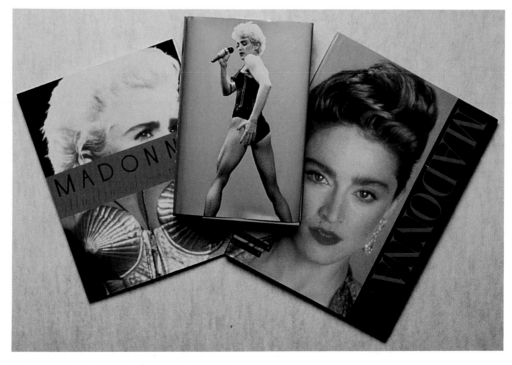

Assorted books, 1990s. $20.00 – 25.00.

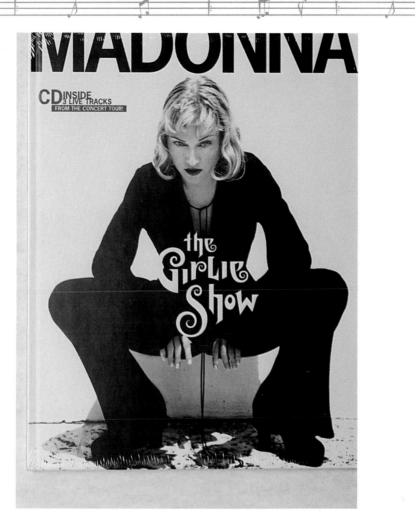

The Girlie Show hardcover book, distributed through fan club, 1994, $45.00 – 65.00.

The controversial Sex book, Warner Bros., 1992. Sealed, $150.00 – 200.00; opened, $50.00 – 75.00.

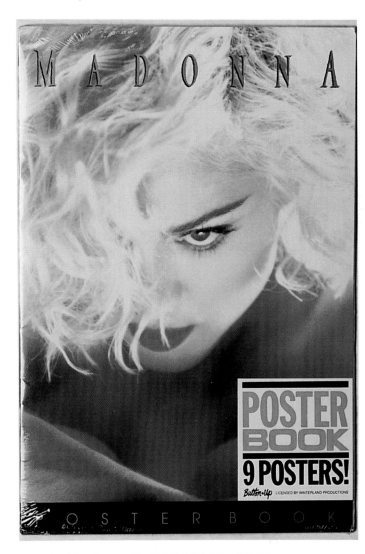

Poster book by Button Up, 1990. $20.00 – 30.00.

"Express Yourself" sports bottle, 1990, Boy Toy. $25.00 – 35.00.

Bumper stickers, top: 1995, Boy Toy, $20.00 – 25.00. Bottom: 1994, MDI, $10.00 – 15.00.

Pinback buttons, Boy Toy, 1986 – 1995. Large, $10.00 – 15.00 each. Button pack, $25.00 – 30.00. Small, $5.00 – 10.00 each.

Calendars. $25.00 – 30.00 each.

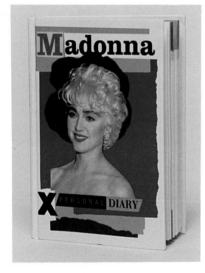

Caps, Boy Toy. 1986 – 1994.
$25.00 – 40.00.

X Personal Diary. $50.00 – 75.00.

CD clock, Playtime, 1994, $50.00 – 75.00. Moving legs clock, unknown manufacturer, 1993, $30.00 – 50.00.

Wrist bands. $30.00 – 40.00.

"Gambler" 45 RPM record with pull-out poster, $15.00 – 20.00.

Concert poster, 1984. Promo poster from first tour, 36" x 24". $50.00 – 75.00.

Fan club postcard set, 1991, Boy Toy. $10.00 – 15.00.

Fan club kit, 1991. $50.00 – 75.00.

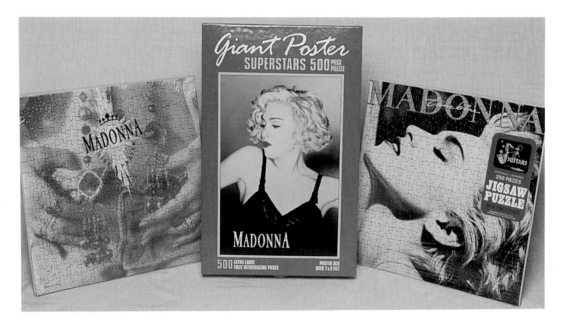

Jigsaw puzzles, left to right: "Like A Prayer," Jigstars, 250 pcs., 1989, $45.00 – 55.00. "Express Yourself," 500 pcs., Milton Bradley, 1990, $25.00 – 45.00. "True Blue" Jigstars, 250 pcs., 1986, $45.00 – 55.00.

Post art portfolio, Boy Toy. $35.00 – 40.00.

Stationery, Star Stationery, 1986. $50.00 – 75.00.

Pogs, Boy Toy, 1992 – 1993. Series 1, $15.00 – 20.00. Series 2, $10.00 – 15.00.

Pillows, both by Boy Toy. Left: "Like A Prayer," 1989. $50.00 – 75.00. Right: Large "Vogue", 1991, $40.00 – 60.00.

Pillow from "Desperately Seeking Susan" movie, 1986. $50.00 – 75.00.

Large mirror. $20.00 – 30.00.

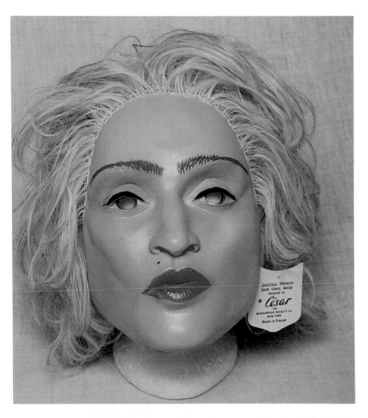

Mask (French), by César for Masquerade Novelty Co., CA, 1989. $175.00 – 225.00.

Waste basket, Boy Toy, 1991, 18", offered through fan club. $150.00 – 175.00.

Assorted keychains, issued 1991 – 1995, Boy Toy. $5.00 – 10.00 each.

Lighter, $20.00 – 30.00. Matches, $5.00 – 10.00.

"Truth or Dare" lamp, Boy Toy, 1992, offered through fan club. $200.00 – 250.00.

Telephone cards, Boy Toy, 1987. $10.00 – 15.00 each.

View-Master gift set, Tyco, from "Dick Tracy" movie, 1990. $20.00 – 25.00.

Wallets. $10.00 – 20.00 each. Far left wallet from the Virgin Tour, 1985, $25.00 – 35.00.

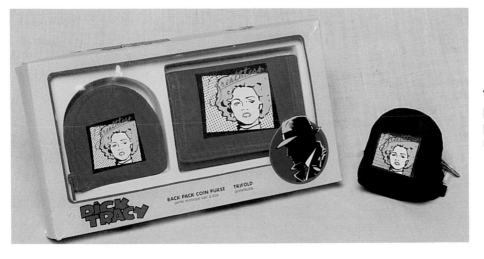

"Breathless" wallet and backpack coin purse set, $25.00 – 35.00. Small backpack keychain, $10.00 – 15.00. Both manufactured 1990.

Watches. Left to right: Nelsonic, 1990, $10.00 – 20.00, Dick Tracy, 1990, $40.00 – 50.00. Fan club, 1991, $30.00 – 40.00.

"Breathless" sock, Pel-Bar Ind., 1990, $35.00 – 50.00. Assorted stickers, 1994, Boy Toy, $5.00 – 10.00 each.

Breathless pouch, $25.00 – 30.00. Breathless fanny pack, $20.00 – 25.00. From "Dick Tracy" movie, 1990.

"Dick Tracy" pillow, from the movie "Dick Tracy," 1990. $20.00 – 30.00.

Breathless figural mug, from "Dick Tracy" movie, manufactured by Applause, 1990. $35.00 – 45.00.

Breathless mug with box, by Applause, from "Dick Tracy" movie, 1990. $35.00 – 45.00.

"Breathless" tumbler, $15.00 – 20.00. "Breathless" canteen, $20.00 – 30.00. "Breathless" mug, $15.00 – 20.00. From "Dick Tracy" movie, 1990.

"Breathless" resin figure, limited edition of 5,000, by Applause, 1990, from "Dick Tracy" movie. $75.00 – 150.00.

"Breathless Mahoney" dolls, Applause, all from "Dick Tracy" movie, 1990. "The Sultry Songstress" doll, 14" by Playmates, $75.00 – 100.00. 12" Breathless doll (standing), $30.00 – 40.00. 9" Breathless doll, $15.00 – 20.00. Breathless PVC figure, $5.00 – 10.00.

Cosmetic glamour set, $40.00 – 60.00. By Cosrich, 1990, from "Dick Tracy" movie.

Jewelry and miscellaneous. Top, left to right: "Vogue" necklace, 1991, Boy Toy, $25.00 – 45.00. "Immaculate" necklace, 1991, Boy Toy, $25.00 – 45.00. "Immaculate" lapel pin, 1991, Boy Toy, $15.00 – 30.00. Bottom, left to right: "Express Yourself" earrings, 1992, Winterland Productions, $25.00 – 45.00. "Breathless" lapel pin, 1990, Gift Creations, $15.00 – 25.00. "Girlie Show" keychain, Viewer 1993, distributed through fan club, $20.00 – 30.00. "Breathless" lapel pin (Dick Tracy), 1990, Applause, $15.00 – 20.00.

Michael Jackson

Learning to sing and dance at a early age was the key to Michael Jackson's musical successes. With his unrelenting desire for perfection throughout his recording career, Michael has understood the chemistry needed to change with the times and reap the benefits of doing so. An unbelievable aspect of Michael is that his singing, dancing popularity, and compassion for others continue to grow.

By the time Michael was 15 years old, he had obtained 13 Top 40 hits with his brothers in the Jackson Five and four Top 40 singles of his own. Michael's career then soared to a level no other musician has been able to match with the release of the "Thriller" album in 1984. The album sold over 40 million copies to become the best selling album of all time.

Due in part to his growing up in the business, Michael has had his share of tabloid gossip, even more it seems than the weekly sightings of the late Elvis Presley. But through it all — fame, fortune, and unprece-dented success, Michael is more than a superstar. His humane nature and willingness to share helped many throughout the world with his support and donations to humanitarian programs.

The Jackson Five's popularity in the early 1970s won them a spot on ABC as an animated cartoon series. The Saturday morning cartoon first aired on September 11, 1971 and ran through September 1, 1973. The Jackson Five also hosted several other musical variety shows on CBS in the mid 1970s.

Since not much was produced, Jackson Five memorabilia is scarce and demands attention. Michael Jackson memorabilia is becoming valuable and is still found commonly at collector shows. Finding memorabilia in excellent to mint condition is important since the higher grades are still in supply at affordable prices and are sure to increase steadily in the future due to Michael's success.

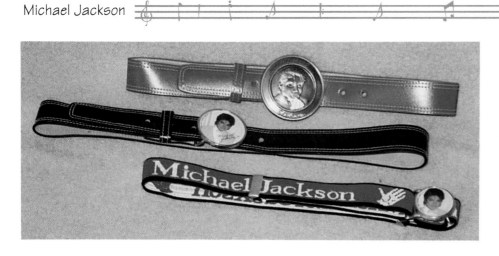

Belts, 1984, US. $20.00 – 30.00 each.

Assorted books. $15.00 – 25.00.

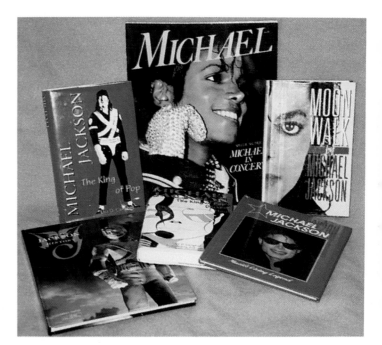

Bumper sticker, $5.00 – 8.00. Back-stage passes, $15.00 – 20.00. Fan club membership cards, $10.00 – 15.00. Bracelet, $10.00 – 15.00. Key ring, $5.00 – 10.00.

Busts. $85.00 – 100.00.

Button set, $15.00 – 20.00. Wallet, $10.00 – 12.00. Watch, $15.00 – 20.00.

Calendar, $20.00 – 30.00. Pencil, $15.00 – 20.00. Cut-out cereal box record, $10.00 – 15.00. Calendar and pencil were offered through fan club.

Pepsi cans, USA, 1984. $10.00 – 15.00. Italy, 1992, $10.00 – 15.00, Center: Michael Raisin, PVC, $40.00 – 45.00.

"Dangerous" record/video store display, 1991, $30.00 – 50.00. Card sets by Topps, $15.00 – 25.00 each. Back stage pass from the "Dangerous" tour, 1991, $25.00 – 30.00.

American Music Awards dolls, Motown, Human Nature, Grammy Awards. 12" by LJN, 1984, $40.00 – 60.00 each .

Dolls: Captain EO Animals, "Hooter" and "Fuzzball," Ideal, 1987. $85.00 – 95.00 each.

Michael's Pets, Ideal 1987. Left to right: "Muscles" the snake, "Cool Bear" (Michael), "Bubbles" the chimp. $80.00 – 90.00 each.

Michael's Pets. Left to right: "Suzie" the rabbit, "Unkle Tookie" the frog, "Lovie" the llama. $80.00 – 90.00 each.

Michael's Pets. Left to right: "Spanky" the dog, "Jeannine" the ostrich, "Mr. Bill" the security dog. $80.00 – 90.00 each.

Michael's Pets, "Jabbar" the giraffe." $80.00 – 90.00.

Hats, $15.00 – 25.00. Socks, $10.00 – 15.00.

Fan club jacket, US. $55.00 – 65.00.

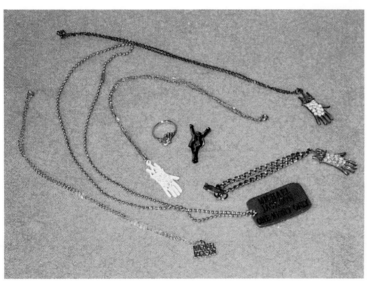

Assorted jewelry, ring, pin, bracelet, necklaces. $10.00 – 15.00 each.

Electronic microphone, 1984, LJN. $40.00 – 45.00.

Assorted perfumes, 1980s.
$35.00 – 50.00.

Pillow, $30.00 – 40.00. Glove,
$10.00 – 15.00.

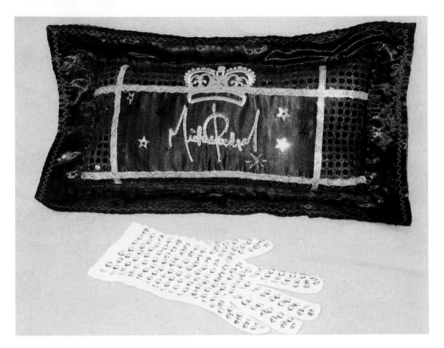

Thriller purse, unlicensed, 1984.
$20.00 – 25.00.

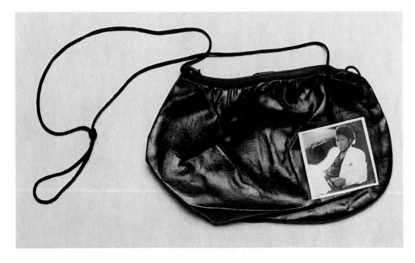

Radio, ERTL, 1984, $25.00 – 30.00. Singalong sound machine, LJN, 1984, $35.00 – 50.00.

Shoes, Billie Jean style, LA Gear. $85.00 – 95.00.

Stamp sets, St. Vincent. $20.00 – 30.00.

View-Master, $15.00 – 20.00. Talking View-Master, $45.00 – 55.00. Talking View-Master viewer, 1984, GAF. $75.00 – 100.00.

The Rolling Stones

According to the 1993 edition of the Guinness Book of World Records, The Rolling Stones have everyone beat when it comes to gold records. The Stones recording totals are 34 gold albums, 15 platinum, and 6 multi-platinum. This shouldn't surprise us since the band has managed to stay together, with some additions and subtractions, longer than any other rock band in history. Their success in the early 1960s built their fame and their popularity continues stronger than ever.

Mick Jagger and Keith Richards first met in primary school at the age of six. It wasn't until 11 years later that they met again through a mutual friend. Both had interests in rhythm and blues and after spending time with other bands in 1962, formed The Rolling Stones including Brian Jones, Ian Stewart, and Dick Taylor. The group got its name from a Muddy Waters song.

The Stones' "Bad Boy" image was a perfect contrast to The Beatles who were dominating the scene of the 1960s. So bad was their image that they had a hard time getting national attention. Ed Sullivan didn't allow them on his show originally because he didn't like their image and didn't want to offend his viewers. It seemed wherever they played, riots ensued.

Ironically, the same image that was so damaging during their early years would actually boost their popularity through time. The Rolling Stones have certainly stood the test of time and have become a household name. Another aspect that has benefited them is their ability to change musically with the times.

Through these long years, lots of Rolling Stones memorabilia has been created. Most however is merchandise from concerts. It is probable that some Rolling Stones items, other than these, from the early years exist. It is likely that most memorabilia featuring The Rolling Stones will be of collectible interest especially when or if the group ever disbands.

Mick Jagger clock, 1980s. $50.00 – 60.00.

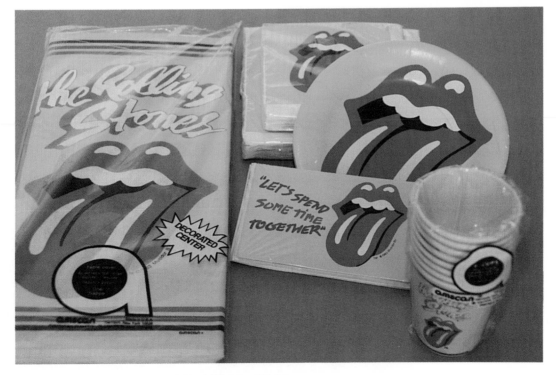

Birthday party set, Musidor, 1983. $60.00 – 70.00.

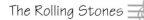

Promotional poster, rare. $750.00 – 1,000.00.

Chu-Bops mini album collection with bubble gum records. 11 records in store display box, Musidor, 1983. $150.00 – 200.00.

Book cover by Musidor, 1981, $10.00 – 15.00. "Tattoo You" spiral notebook and school folder by Musidor, 1981, $10.00 – 15.00. "Steel Wheels" tour license plate, 1989, $10.00 – 15.00. Sticker collector's album by Musidor, 1983, $10.00 – 15.00.

Barrette, $10.00 – 12.00. Earrings, $10.00 – 12.00. Assorted keychains, 1983, $10.00 – 15.00.

3-D glasses, store promotion for "Steel Wheels" tour TV special, 1990, $20.00 – 30.00. Air freshener, Medo, 1983, $10.00 – 15.00.

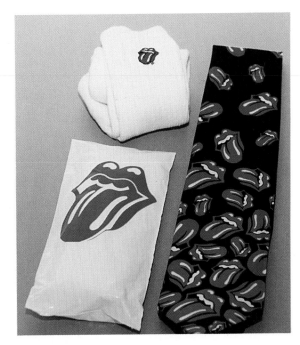

Dolls, 1963, mfg. by Play Pals, rare, a set of five was made. $250.00 – 300.00 each.

Socks, $10.00 – 20.00. Poncho, $15.00 – 20.00. Tie, $30.00 – 40.00. All by Brockum, 1994.

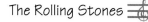

Pinback buttons, 1970s – 1980s. Small, $3.00 – 5.00. Large, $4.00 – 8.00.

Self-stick seals, Absca, 1983, $10.00 – 25.00 each. RAD A-Tattoos, Brockam, 1991, $10.00 – 25.00 each. Puffy stickers, Musidor, 1983, $10.00 – 15.00 each, sealed.

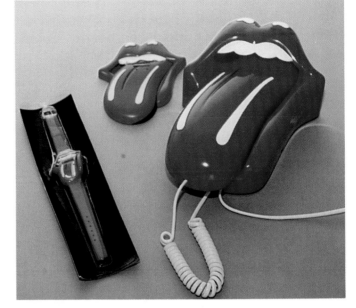

Watch, $50.00 – 75.00. Clock, $50.00 – 75.00. Phone, $100.00 – 150.00. All by Musidor, 1983.

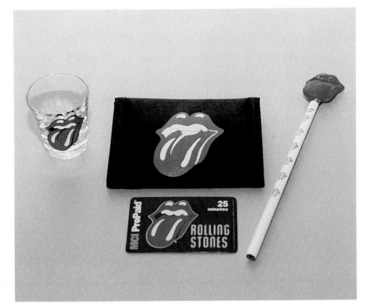

Shot glass, $15.00 – 30.00. Wallet, $10.00 – 15.00. Phone card, $10.00 – 15.00. Pencil, $5.00 – 10.00. All items, 1994.

Flashpoint matches, $5.00 – 10.00. Incense holder, $35.00 – 50.00. Air fresheners, Medo, 1983, $10.00 – 15.00

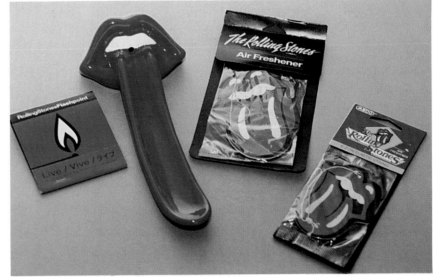

"Shmuzzle" jigsaw puzzle, Musidor, 1983.
$50.00 – 75.00.

Voodoo Lounge tour items. Scarf, $10.00 – 15.00.
Ashtray, $10.00 – 15.00. Pin, $10.00 – 15.00.
Keychain viewers, $5.00 – 10.00. Decal, $5.00 –
10.00. Cup, $10.00 – 15.00. All items, 1994.

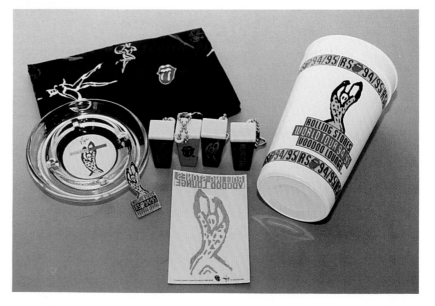

Watch, $35.00 – 45.00. Alarm clock, $40.00 –
50.00. Dollar bill, $5.00 – 8.00. Patch, $5.00 –
8.00. 1994.

The Bee Gees

Five members originally made up The Bee Gees when they made their debut in America. Two members left and the three remaining brothers made history. The Bee Gees enjoyed success in the late 1960s and 1970s with a string of hits. It wasn't until the release of the movie soundtrack "Saturday Night Fever" in 1977 that the group rocketed to superstar status. Though many groups contested them, The Bee Gees were then the undisputed kings of the disco era and the "Fever" soundtrack and film came to be known as the pinnacle of the disco movement.

Disco was the creation of fast beating music, lights, glittered clothing, and above all DANCE. Nightclubs popped up all across the nation. Disco dance lessons were taught, dance clothes sold, and merchandise was created to accommodate the fad. Historically, disco was a fusion of what pop music had turned into: a metamorphosis across time. The important factor is that for the first time, dance played a major role in music. This would be the founding and

stepping stone for most pop music.

Andy Gibb was another important player in this era and as a brother of the Bee Gees deserves mention here. Andy enjoyed super stardom as a solo act and had five gold hits, three of which were number one singles. Andy, unlike his brothers, successfully chose slower songs without the fast disco beat for his audience. He was also considered a sex symbol among his young audience.

The merchandise issued for The Bee Gees and Andy is for the most part still available at reasonable prices. But after Andy's death in 1987, the Andy Gibb doll doubled in price. The Bee Gees lunchboxes have increased sharply in value also. This increase, however, has been mainly fueled by the increased interest in lunchboxes by collectors. Other Bee Gees merchandise represents not only a group but the era of disco music. For this reason, more than just rock-n-roll collectors are interested in their merchandise.

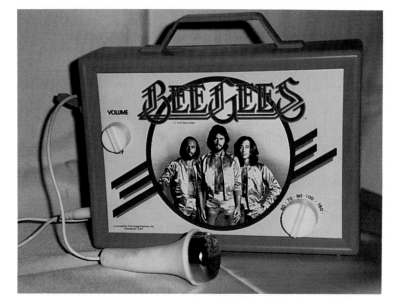

Amp and microphone, The Image Factory, 1979. $100.00 – 125.00.

Backpack, The Image Factory, 1978. $50.00 – 75.00.

Belt buckle, unknown manufacturer, 1979. $25.00 – 35.00

"The Legend: The Illustrated Story of the Bee Gees," by David English. Volume I, $75.00 – 80.00. Volume 2, $100.00 – 115.00.

Music books. "Living Eyes," $25.00 – 35.00. "Bee Gees Greatest," $40.00 – 50.00. "Main Course," $30.00 – 40.00. "Bee Gees Anthology," $35.00 – 45.00. "Bee Gees 1975 – 1978," $40.00 – 50.00. "Bee Gees Spirits Having Flown," $35.00 – 45.00. Vol. 1, $40.00. Vol. 2, $50.00 – 60.00.

Books. "Sgt. Pepper's Lonely Hearts Club Band, The Movie." Scrapbook, $75.00 – 95.00. Storybook, $40.00 – 50.00.

1979 Bee Gees Fan Club Kit. Came with bio, four color 8 x 10s, membership certificate, order forms, and 45 single with personal message. $75.00 – 100.00.

1980 Andy Gibb Official Fan Club folder, bio, 8 x 10, iron-on, update membership certificate, and order forms. $100.00 – 125.00.

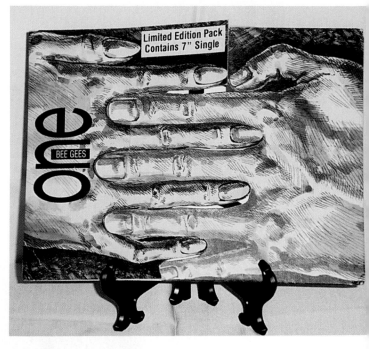

"One," hand pack. Import from Germany, limited edition. $40.00 – 50.00.

Magazines. Bee Gees, *Rolling Stone* Covers. 1976: White Shirts, $25.00 – 30.00. 1978, Sgt. Pepper, $15.00 – 20.00. 1979, Black and white, $30.00 – 40.00.

Mirror, Sgt. Pepper, $50.00 – 60.00. Mirror with logo and picture, $25.00 – 30.00. Mirror, logo only, $35.00 – 40.00.

1979 *TV Guide*, Bee Gees on cover (promoting "Bee Gees Special" on NBC, Nov. 15, 1979). $25.00 – 30.00.

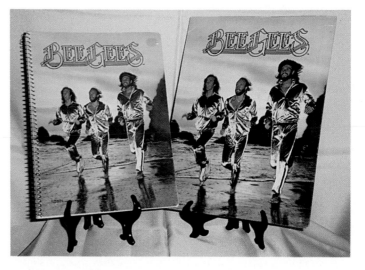

Spiral notebook by Rock On, 1979, $35.00 – 45.00. School folder by Rock On, 1979, $25.00 – 35.00.

"Bee Gees Greatest" mobile, promotional for album, 1979, rare. $125.00 – 150.00.

Patches, 1979, blue with yellow logo (European), $20.00 – 25.00.
Bee Gees logo fan club issue, $35.00 – 40.00.

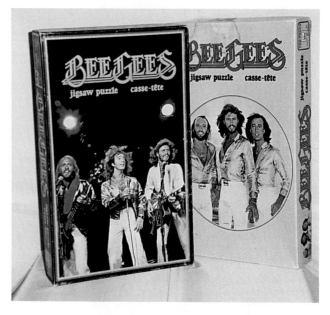

Jigsaw puzzles, APC, 1978 – 1979. $30.00 – 45.00 each.

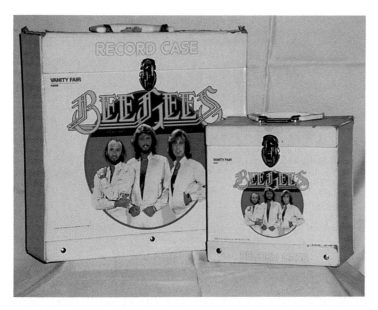

Record cases, both by Vanity Fair, 1979. Left: For LPS, $50.00 –
75.00. Right: For 45RPM, $40.00 – 50.00.

Bee Gees/Sgt. Pepper movie trash can, 1978, The
Stigwood Group. $50.00 – 60.00.

1979 T-shirts. Promotional shirt for "Legend" book, $30.00 – 40.00. '79 Tour jersey, $25.00 – 35.00. French knit, $30.00 – 40.00.

1980 Andy Gibb Official Fan Club folder, bio, 8" x 10", iron-on, update membership certificate, and order forms. $100.00 – 125.00.

1978 Andy Gibb jigsaw puzzles, The Stigwood Group. $15.00 – 25.00 each.

Andy Gibb spiral notebook by Rock On, 1979, $45.00 – 60.00.
School folder by Rock On, 1979, $30.00 – 50.00.

Andy Gibb beach towel, 1978, The Stigwood Group.
$50.00 – 60.00.

Andy Gibb's private photo album, send-away,
1978, Tigerbeat. $15.00 – 20.00.

Andy Gibb microphone by LJN, 1978.
$40.00 – 75.00.

Hammer

With rap music gaining popularity in America came the need to crown a king. In perfect time came Hammertime! Hammer, born Stanley Kirk Burrell in 1962, was the most celebrated rap music star to date. His flashy fast-paced dance routines and clever blend of past hits with bouncy rap mixes won him superstar success in the rap circuit.

Hammer began as M.C. Hammer (M.C. stood for Master of Ceremonies) and through time dropped the M.C., becoming just Hammer. At a young age Hammer was a bat boy for a professional baseball team. After a time in the service and an unsuccessful attempt at college, Hammer began his rap and dance routine in the Bay Area club scene. After some success Hammer convinced two old friends from his baseball years to invest in him so he could start his own record label. With this secured, Hammer recorded an album and sold the LP from the trunk of his car. With the success of his album sales came an interest from Capitol Records. His rise to the top came quickly.

His "Hammer, Don't Hurt 'Em" album sold five million copies in a few short months. After this success came three Grammy awards and five American Music awards. The album was the first rap album in history to create three Top 10 hits on the pop charts.

Hammer's ultimate clean-cut success won him a short lived animated cartoon series on ABC-TV in 1990. Along with his younger audience came a huge amount of youngster-related Hammer memorabilia. Everything was created from dolls and puzzles to a whole string of school supplies. Much of Hammer's merchandise is still available through the collectors circuit. Because of his popularity, Hammer memorabilia is certain to appreciate in value with the generation that adored him.

Bubble gum pouch and bubble gum folder, Rock Express, 1991. $8.00 – 12.00 each.

Clothing patterns, Simplicity, 1991. $10.00 – 15.00 each.

Doll with cassette, Mattel, 1991. $20.00 – 30.00.

Glass picture, unlicensed piece, 1990. $10.00 – 15.00.

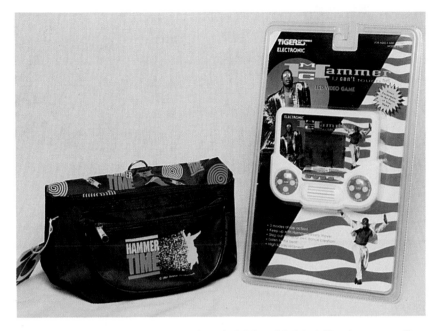

Fanny pack, Bustin' Productions, 1991, $15.00 – 20.00. LCD video game, Tiger Electronics, 1991, $20.00 – 35.00.

School folders, Bustin' Productions, 1991. $10.00 – 15.00 each.

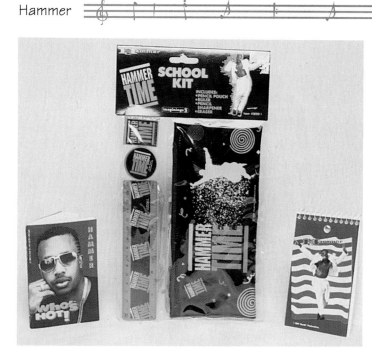

School kit, $20.00 – 25.00. Notebook, $5.00 – 10.00. Booklet $5.00 – 10.00. All by Bustin' Productions, 1991.

View-Master gift set, $20.00 – 25.00. View-Master, $10.00 – 15.00. By Tyco, 1991.

Vinyl wallet, nylon wallet, Bustin' Productions, 1991. $25.00 – 30.00 each.

New Kids On The Block

Not since The Beatles had any rock-n-roll group been able to create the same emotional euphoria with fans. For nearly 20 years, countless teen idols, gimmicks and styles tried but none could match the Fab Four phenomenon.

Then came the New Kids On The Block. Sure, they didn't write songs or play instruments like the Fab Four but a young '80s generation didn't care.

By the powers of the group's creator, Maurice Starr, (ex New Edition), Danny, Donny, Joe, Jordan and Jonathan (brothers) were transformed into superstars. The members were recruited by Starr's talent scout and spent four years developing their act.

In the summer of 1988, the Kids (none over age 20) toured with teen-queen Tiffany and instantly became successful. All members became idols through the teeny-bop circuit. Primarily a rap music act, The Kids wowed their fans with their polished singing and dancing abilities. Much of their success was due in part to the incorporation of dance into pop music and the popularity of rap music. The New Kids, like other successful acts before them, also had an animated cartoon show on Saturday mornings. In light of their popularity with the young pop audience, the New Kids marketed everything.

A huge flood of items was created, marketed, and sold. Their total merchandise sales was in the neighborhood of 400 million dollars in 1990. Some of the items produced are still available in stores today if one is lucky enough to find them. Due to the band's incredible popularity, these items are worthy of investment for the future collectors of music memorabilia. Many items disappeared almost as fast as they were produced. Some items like the New Kids suspenders, shoelaces, and keychain viewers are certain to become rare and of higher value due to their unusual nature and market scarcity.

Binders, Imaginings, 1989. $10.00 – 15.00 each.

Backpack, Big Step Productions, 1990, USA. $15.00 – 20.00.

Bubble gum cassettes by Topps, 1990, set of 24. Full box of cassettes with box, $50.00 – 60.00.

Sports bottle, $5.00 – 10.00. Mug, $5.00 – 10.00. Both by Big Step Productions, 1989.

Bubble gum cards. Display box, $20.00 – 25.00. Each pack, $2.00 – 2.50. By Topps, 1990.

Button set, 1990, Big Step Productions. $5.00 – 10.00.

Cassette tape player, Big Step Productions, 1990, $30.00 – 40.00. Radio, Big Step Productions, 1990, $30.00 – 40.00.

Deluxe Colorforms, Colorforms, 1991. $10.00 – 15.00.

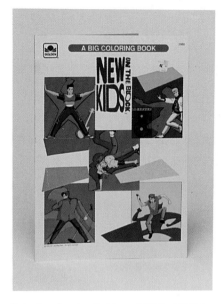

Coloring book, Golden, 1990. $5.00 – 8.00.

Showtime Kids dolls, 18", Hasbro, 1990, $25.00 – 30.00 each.

In Concert dolls, Hasbro, 1990. $20.00 – 25.00 each.

Hangin' Loose dolls, 12", Hasbro, 1990. $25.00 – 30.00 each.

Small poseable dolls, Hasbro, 1990. $5.00 – 10.00 each.

Card game, 1990, Milton Bradley. $15.00 – 20.00.

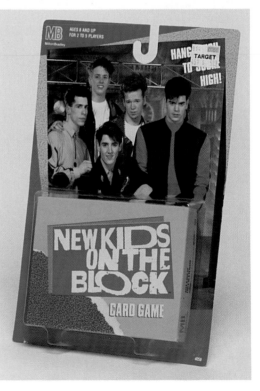

143

Board game, Milton Bradley, 1990. $15.00 – 25.00.

Keychain, Winterland Productions, 1990, $5.00 – 10.00. Yo-yo, Spectra Star, 1990, $10.00 – 15.00. Viewer, Rock Express, 1990, $15.00 – 20.00.

Fashion plates, Hasbro, 1990. $30.00 – 40.00.

Jigsaw puzzles, Milton Bradley, 1990. $10.00 – 15.00 each.

500-piece jigsaw puzzles, Milton Bradley. $10.00 – 15.00 each.

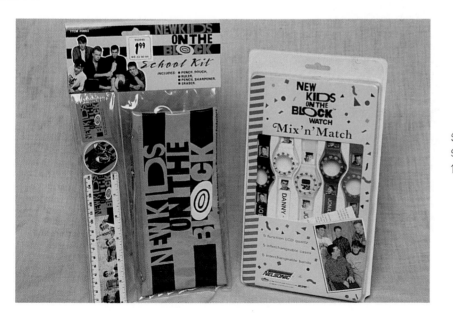

School kit, Big Step Productions, 1990, $15.00 – 20.00. Watch set, Nelsonic, 1990, $15.00 – 20.00.

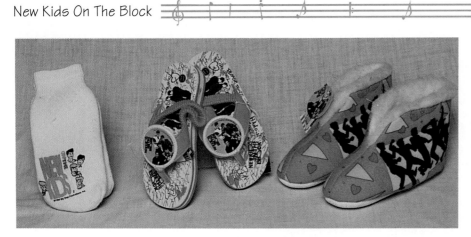

Socks, $10.00 – 15.00. Thongs, $15.00 – 20.00. Slippers, $15.00 – 20.00. All by Big Step Productions, 1990.

Stage set, Hasbro, 1990. $30.00 – 40.00.

Telephone, $20.00 – 30.00. Microphone, $20.00 – 30.00. Both by Big Step Productions, 1990.

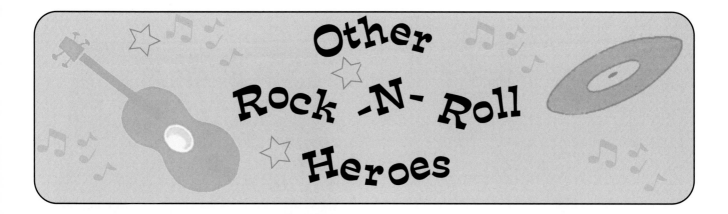

Other Rock -N- Roll Heroes

Through the years nearly every rock-n-roll (or pop) group of any marketing importance has created some sort of collectible memorabilia. Groups with a hit song produced a single. This single in most cases produced an album. If the group went on tour to promote the album, chances are tour guides and t-shirts at the very least were marketed.

Many companies realizing the tremendous potential in merchandising began creating memorabilia to target the young music fans. Before you knew it, a wide variety of music memorabilia was in every store in the country. Dolls, puzzles, games, and jewelry items were just the beginning. But for many lesser known artists it was the beginning and the end. This was due largely to test marketing by companies to see what the market would accept. If these test items sold well, others would be created and marketed.

The artist's appeal to the younger set also denoted how much merchandise was to be produced. If the appeal was enormous, so was the amount of memorabilia manufactured. This chapter focuses on the memorabilia that was created by other rock-n-roll heroes. Since less of these items were produced, this usually places the items into a higher value category. This is due also to the items' obscurity. Many items found in this chapter are of considerable value due to their scarcity in the market place. Finding any of these items is usually based upon luck. Finding them in excellent to mint condition is even rarer. Some of the most interesting, collectible, and rare rock-n-roll treasures are featured in this chapter.

Bad Company mirror, 12" x 12", 1979. $20.00 – 25.00.

AC/DC promotional store display, signed by Malcolm Young, US, mfg. by Atlantic Records, $100.00 – 125.00.

Badfinger, Japanese white-label promo copy of the Iveys "Maybe Tomorrow" L.P. The Iveys later became Badfinger. Rare. $800.00 – 1,000.00.

The Allman Brothers, promotional mobile, "Wipe the Windows, Check the Oil," US, $75.00 – 100.00.

Bangles clock, $50.00 – 75.00. Promotional calendars, 1986, $40.00 – 50.00.

Badfinger, the ultra-rare cover slick of the U.S. unreleased Iveys L.P. "Maybe Tomorrow." The Iveys later became Badfinger. $500.00 – 700.00.

Blondie, miscellaneous promotional items. $40.00 – 100.00 each.

James Brown "Cookeez" brand cookies. Four types were produced, French Vanilla Creameez, Chocolate Chip Feel Goodeez, Chocolate Sandwich Creameez, Banana Peanut Butter Creameez, 1990. $15.00 – 20.00.

Culture Club/Boy George "In His Own Words" book, Omnibus, 1983, $15.00 – 20.00. Puffy stickers, 1984, $10.00 – 15.00. Keychain, 1984, $5.00 – 10.00.

Culture Club pinback buttons, large, $6.00 – 8.00. Small, $3.00 – 5.00.

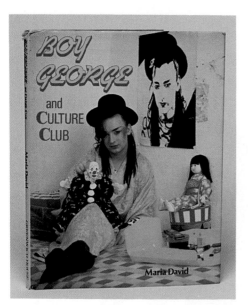

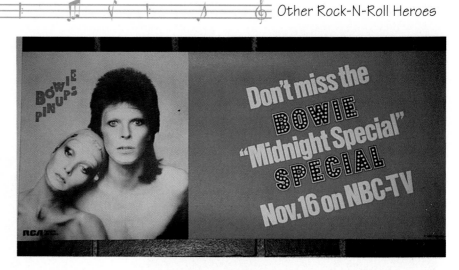

David Bowie, promotional poster, US, 1973. $150.00 – 250.00.

Boy George & Culture Club hardcover book, Greenwich House, 1984. $15.00 – 20.00.

Dick Clark tie clip, $45.00 – 55.00. Cufflinks, on original "American Bandstand" card, 1958, $75.00 – 95.00.

Bobby Darin "Scripto" ink pen on original display card with record, 1958. $85.00 – 100.00.

Bob Dylan, early promotional poster with Dylan artwork, US, 1966, CBS Records. $400.00 – 600.00.

Elton John promotional poster for "Don't Shoot Me I'm Only the Piano Player" LP, 1972, US, MCA Records. $250.00 – 400.00.

Heart "Dog and Butterfly" music box, 1978, rare. $150.00 – 200.00.

Heart "Even It Up" sheet music, 1980 Warner Bros. "Dog & Butterfly" sheet music, 1978, Warner Bros. $8.00 – 12.00.

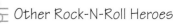

Heart, playing cards, 1990. $40.00 – 50.00.

"All I Wanna Do" perfume, rare. $50.00 – 75.00.

Jimi Hendrix, personal water pipe and scales. $8,000.00 – 10,000.00.

Jimi Hendrix, Gold Record Award for "Band of Gypsys" LP, US,
Capitol Records. $3,000.00 – 5,000.00.

Buddy Holly, shirt, 1958, personally owned and worn by Buddy, includes a picture of him
wearing the shirt. $2,500.00 – 3,500.00.

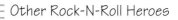

Buddy Holly, personal items, high school years, moccasins, shoes, belt, hunting bag, 1955 – 1957, $500.00 – 1,000.00 each.

Led Zeppelin, inflatable promo blimp distributed to music stores for record promotion, $100.00 – 200.00. Sew-on patch, $5.00 – 10.00.

Led Zeppelin, fan club 8 x 10 photo, 1973, $15.00 – 20.00. Mirror, $10.00 – 15.00. Pinback buttons, issued in 1970s. $5.00 – 8.00 each.

Jimmy Page's leather jacket, circa 1970, $1,000.00 – 1,500.00.

John Lennon, long-sleeved shirt, 1970s, and a picture of John wearing it. $3,000.00 – 4,000.00.

John Lennon, 1974, US, Wall and Bridges promotional items. $20.00 – 40.00 each.

John Lennon and Yoko Ono, running suits, 1970. $3,000.00 – 5,000.00.

John Lennon's t-shirt, "This Is Not Here." $3,000.00 – 5,000.00.

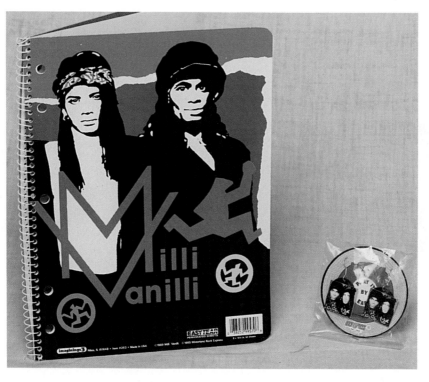

Milli Vanilli, notebook, $10.00 – 15.00. Earrings, $10.00 – 15.00. Both 1989, Winterland Productions.

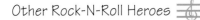
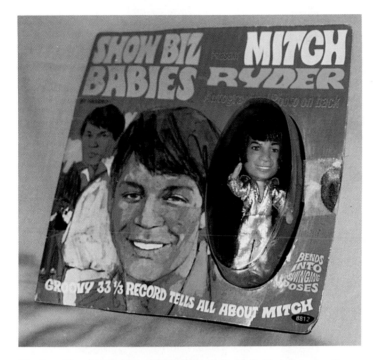

Hasbro Showbiz Babies, 1967, "Mitch Ryder," 4" doll, loose & complete, $100.00 – 150.00. Carded, $300.00 – 350.00. Rarer than the other Showbiz Babies.

Hasbro Showbiz Babies, 1967 "Spencer Davis", 4" doll, loose & complete, $75.00 – 100.00. Carded, $250.00 – 350.00.

Nelson jigsaw puzzle, 100 pcs., Milton Bradley, 1991, $10.00 – 15.00. Gum folder, 1991, $8.00 – 12.00. Gum pouch, 1991, $8.00 – 12.00.

Pointer Sisters' personally painted Reebok sneakers, 1990, done for a charity auction. $300.00 – 500.00 pair.

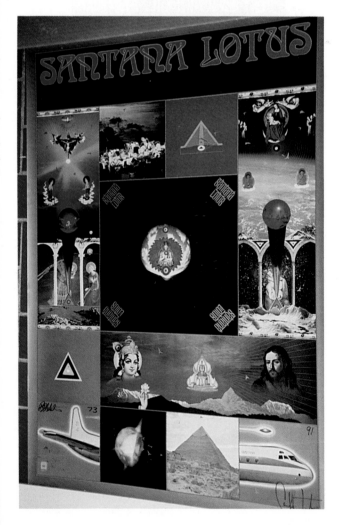

Santana, promotional poster signed by Carlos Santana. $200.00 – 300.00.

Stevie Nicks' hat, signed by Stevie, late 1980s, personally owned and stage worn. $750.00 – 1,000.00.

Cat Stevens, promo Frisbee, 1980s. $10.00 – 15.00,

Tiny Tim, "Of Beautiful Things" board game, Parker Brothers, 1970. $100.00 – 175.00.

Stevie Ray Vaughan, promotional poster, mid-1980s, signed by Stevie. $500.00 – 600.00.

Village People, toy guitar, 36", Carnival Toys, 1978. $100.00 – 200.00. Jigsaw puzzle, APC, 1978, $60.00 – 90.00.

Vanilla Ice, 12" dolls, THQ, 1991. $35.00 – 40.00.

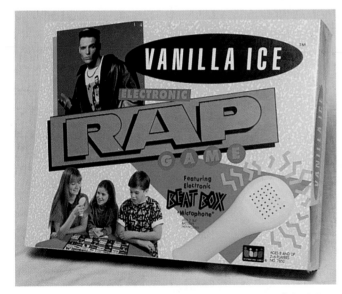

Vanilla Ice, Rap Game, International Games, 1991. $75.00 – 100.00.

Vanilla Ice, bubble gum cassettes, Topps, 1991. Full box, $75.00 – 90.00. Each, $1.00 – 2.00.

The Concert Scene

The roots of all rock-n-roll memorabilia are in the music itself. Live concerts provide proof to best exemplify this fact. Nothing is more satisfying than hearing your favorite musician perform live in concert. In some cases for the entertainer and ticket holder, this excursion is a one-time event. But perhaps equally as exciting as seeing your idol live is to take home a piece of the show. This chapter catalogs some of the many items created to promote the concert scene.

Concert posters and advertising flyers are the first items created and displayed in the promotion of a concert. A sampling of the thousands produced through the years are pictured here. Posters and flyers have a certain nostalgic quality to them. Depending on the entertainer and the show, some have considerable value as well.

Concert tickets and ticket stubs are certainly a collectible item. Again, depending on the performer and the show, these may fetch a high market value for collectors. This single item is often the only memento a person has from a show.

Tour programs and guides are one of the most common items created and distributed at various shows. Tour programs were limited in production. Generally a new one was created to promote each tour. Some tour guides due to show circumstances (i.e., a famous appearance, first or last performance) are of significant value today. Tour programs in general are rather scarce due to the simple fact that many concert goers never purchased one. Some tour programs are extremely plentiful, such as the Beatles 1964 and 1965 USA Ltd programs; a warehouse find of these two programs occurred some years back. Because of this, their value has not grown past the $50 mark.

Other concert memorabilia in general is rare due to its limited production and distribution at shows. An item's uniqueness usually denotes its value.

Finally, a collection of photos has been gathered here of several one-of-a-kind items. These pieces were used as props or stage suits or are personal effects.

Eric Clapton, personally
owned stage outfit, 1980s,
designed by Johnny Versace.
$2,000.00 – 2,500.00.

Guns 'n Roses, drum head, 1989,
used on tour, one of the first logos
used by the band, one of a kind.
$2,500.00 – 3,500.00.

Guns 'n Roses, tour jacket signed by
the band, donated by charity auction.
$600.00 – 750.00.

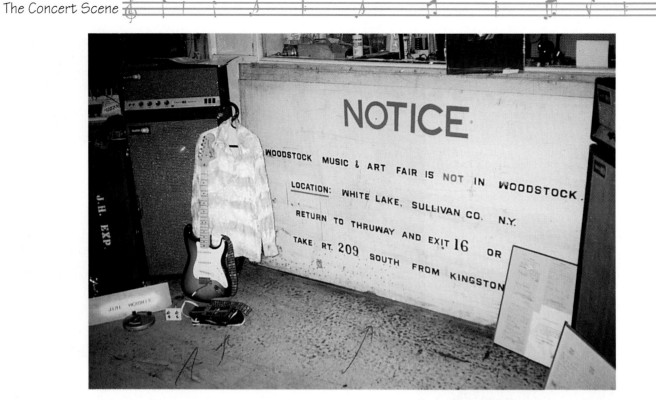

A road sign for the 1969 Woodstock concert. $4,000.00 – 5,000.00. Jimi Hendrix's guitar, last one he bought at Manny's on 48th St. in N.Y.C. The receipt for the guitar reflects its serial number and was signed for by Jimi's last road manager. The receipt was dated 2 months before his death. Jimi played this Fender guitar at the opening party of the Electric Lady Studios in NYC and on his last L.P., "Cry of Love." Guitar: $100,000.00 – 125,000.00. Stage outfit, $15,000.00 – 20,000.00. Amps, $10,000.00 – 12,000.00.

Michael Jackson, concert tour t-shirt, 1994. $20.00 – 25.00.

Michael Jackson concert tour t-shirt, $20.00 – 25.00. 1994.

Joan Jett, stage outfit, 1980, owned and worn by Joan. $600.00 – 900.00.

Led Zeppelin, 1977 tour t-shirt (last US tour), from concert in Oakland, California, July 1977. $50.00 – 75.00.

Led Zeppelin, 1977 tour t-shirt (last US tour). $50.00 – 75.00.

Madonna, backstage passes, assorted concerts, 1985 – 1992. $20.00 – 30.00 each.

Madonna, tour bandanna, "Blonde Ambition" tour, 1990. $30.00 – 50.00.

Madonna, "Blonde Ambition" tour jacket (back), 1990. $200.00 – 250.00.

Madonna tour laminates, assorted concerts, 1985 – 1992. $10.00 – 20.00 each.

Stevie Nicks, "Butterfly" cape, 1980s, custom designed and personally owned and stage worn by Stevie. $1,500.00 – 2,000.00.

Pink Floyd, 35' long, 18' tall inflatable pig used on their "Momentary Lapse of Reason" tour, 1987. $6,000.00 – 8,000.00.

Van Halen, tour jackets, 1984. $200.00 – 300.00 each.

Concert flyer for the Animals 1966 tour. $50.00 – 75.00.

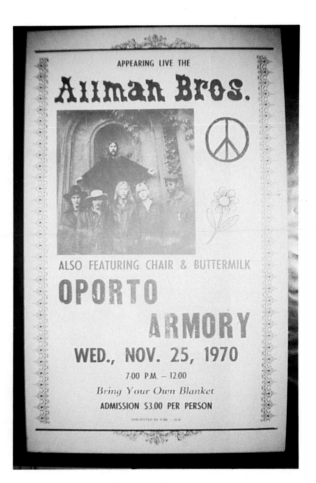

The Allman Brothers, early 1970s concert poster. $500.00 – 600.00.

Badfinger, concert poster. $150.00 – 200.00.

Beach Boys, concert poster, July 2, 1966. $1,500.00 – 2,000.00.

Beatles, concert poster for Shea Stadium, 8/23/66 show, very rare. $10,000.00 – 12,000.00.

Beatles, concert poster for Candlestick Park, 8/29/66 show, their last concert. $1,500.00 – 2,500.00.

The Beatles, 1961, River Mersey, UK, rare. $5,000.00 – 7,000.00.

The Beatles, Liverpool, 1961, UK, the same week Brian Epstein saw the Beatles for the first time, rare. $5,000.00 – 7,000.00.

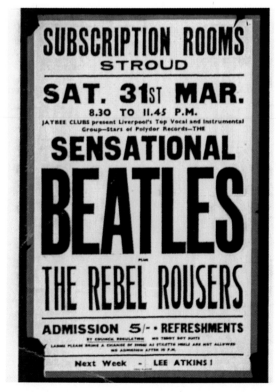

The Beatles, Stroud, UK, 1962, rare. $5,000.00 – 7,000.00.

The Beatles, Liverpool, 1962, UK, note misspelled "BEETLES," rare. $5,000.00 – 7,000.00.

The Beatles, Liverpool, 1962, UK, historic meeting between John Lennon and Delbert McClinton which resulted in the harmonica riff on "Love Me Do," "From Me to You," and "Please Please Me." Rare. $5,000.00 – 7,000.00.

The Beatles, Liverpool, 1963, UK, rare. $4,000.00 – 5,000.00.

Chuck Berry and Canned Heat, mid-1970s, US. $75.00 – 150.00.

Big Brother & The Holding Company, concert poster, 1971. $125.00 – 250.00.

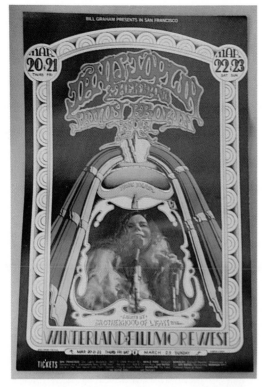

Big Brother and The Holding Company, Fillmore West concert poster. $750.00 – 1,000.00.

Big Brother and The Holding Company, concert poster. $500.00 – 600.00.

Early Alice Cooper concert poster, 1969. $100.00 – 150.00.

Jackson Browne, San Jose, 1976, US. $200.00 – 250.00.

Canned Heat, Boston, 1970, US. $75.00 – 150.00.

The Byrds, Fillmore East, 1969, US. $250.00 – 300.00.

Harry Chapin, N.Y., 1974, US. $150.00 – 200.00.

Commander Cody and the Lost Planet Airmen, Seattle, 1975, US. $100.00 – 150.00.

173

Deep Purple and The Guess Who, concert poster, 1969. $50.00 – 100.00.

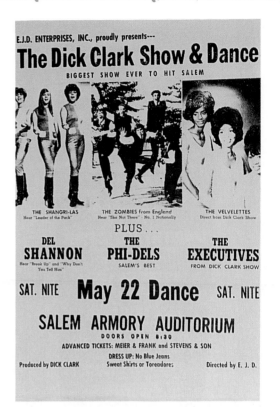

Dick Clark Show 1965 poster. $60.00 – 75.00.

The Doors, Santa Barbara, 1968, US. $750.00 – 1,000.00.

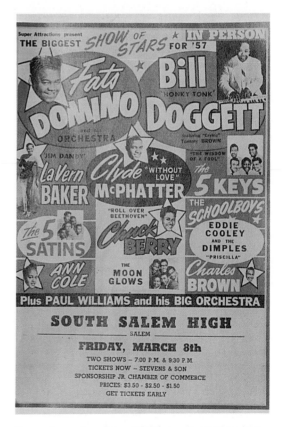

Concert poster from 1957. Look at this lineup (and prices!). $800.00 – 1,000.00.

Original large metal sign that hung in front of the Fillmore East Concert Hall until 1971. $8,000.00 – 10,000.00.

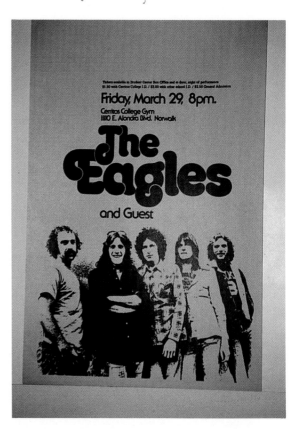

The Eagles, Cerritos College, 1973, US. $250.00 – 350.00.

1964 concert poster featuring Billy Fury. $150.00 – 200.00.

The Jackson Five, concert poster, Feb. 13, 1971.
$700.00 – 800.00.

Heart/Cheap Trick, 1990 tour poster. $10.00 –
15.00.

Jethro Tull with Joe Cocker and Fleetwood Mac,
Houston, 1970, US. $200.00 – 250.00.

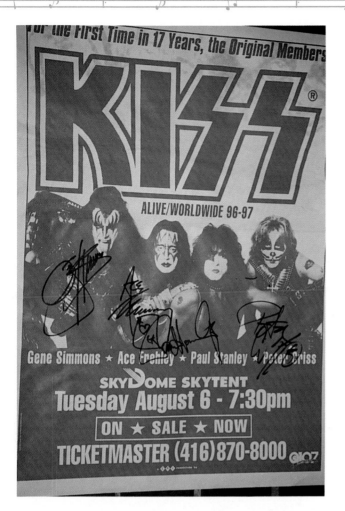

Gladys Knight and the Pips were the headline of this 1965 concert, mfg. by Globe Poster Co. $1,000.00 – 1,500.00.

Kiss, 1996, US, autographed by the band. $150.00 – 250.00.

Led Zeppelin, Earl's Court, London, UK, rare. $1,000.00 – 1,250.00.

Led Zeppelin and others, Dallas, 1970, US. $600.00 – 700.00.

Little Richard, concert poster in Salem, Oregon, 1958. $300.00 – 500.00.

Madonna, "Blond Ambition" tour poster, 1990. $30.00 – 50.00.

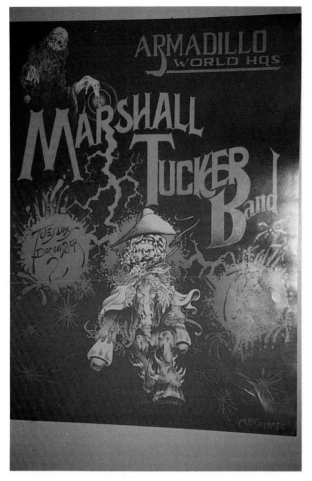

Marshall Tucker Band, Austin, 1973, US. $75.00 – 100.00.

Rick Nelson, concert poster, 1970. $150.00 – 200.00.

Pink Floyd, 1967 concert poster, English.
$750.00 – 1,000.00.

Pink Floyd, concert poster at the Fillmore. $500.00 –
600.00.

Paul Revere & The Raiders, concert poster. $40.00 –
50.00.

Sonny & Cher, 1965 flyer. $50.00 – 75.00.

Steve Miller, St. Louis, 1969, US. $150.00 – 250.00.

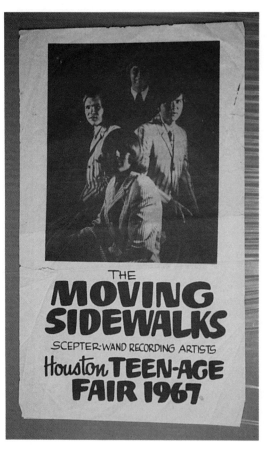

The Moving Sidewalks, Billy Gibbons of ZZ Top, Houston, 1967, US, handbill. $130.00 – 150.00.

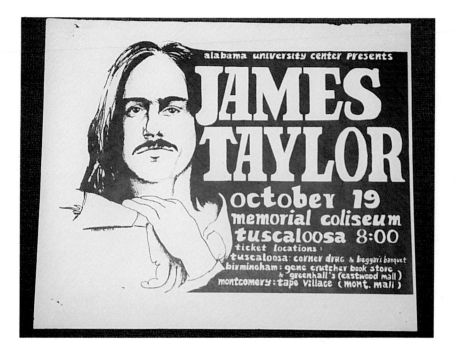

James Taylor, Tuscaloosa, 1972, US. $100.00 – 150.00.

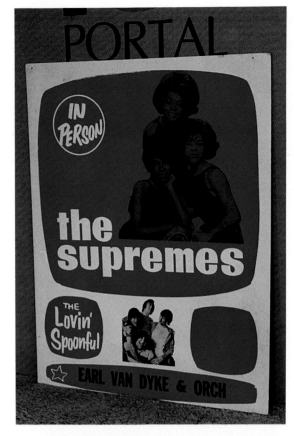

The Supremes, 1960s handbill from Chapel Hill, University of North Carolina. $500.00 – 600.00.

Turtles, show flyer 1966, the only major tour with all six original Turtles. $25.00 – 35.00.

The Vanilla Fudge, concert flyer, New Year's Day, 1969. $20.00 – 30.00.

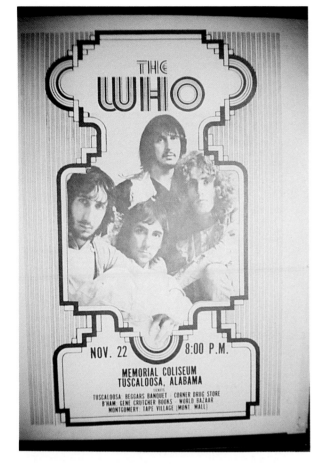

The Who, early 1970s concert poster. $400.00 – 500.00.

The Who, Fillmore East, 1969, US. $150.00 – 250.00.

Concert flyer for "The Yardbirds" 1966 tour. By the time this poster was printed, Jimmy Page had joined the band. At this particular show, Jeff Beck had already quit. $100.00 – 150.00.

The Young Rascals, concert flyer, 1967. $30.00 – 50.00.

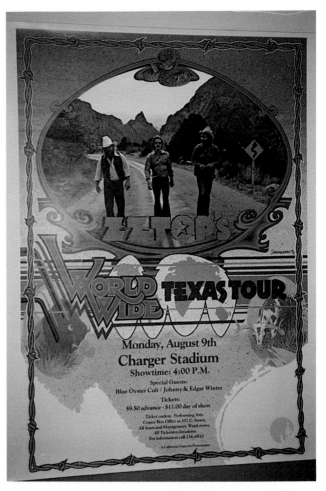

ZZ Top, San Diego, 1973, US. $100.00 – 150.00.

The Beach Boys, tour program, 1976. $25.00 – 30.00.

Cheap Trick "Dream Police," tour program, 1979. $20.00 – 30.00.

Eric Clapton, tour program, 1988. $25.00 – 35.00.

Alice Cooper, tour program. $25.00 – 30.00.

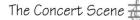

Crosby, Stills, Nash & Young, tour program, 1974, the only tour with all four members since 1970. $30.00 – 40.00.

John Denver tour program, 1980. $15.00 – 20.00.

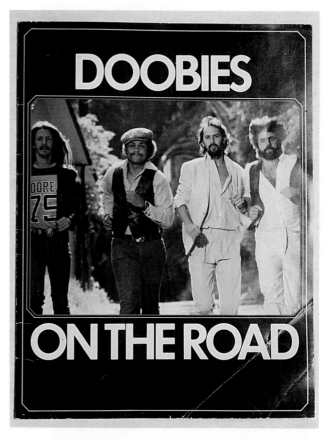

Doobie Brothers, "Takin' It To The Streets" tour program, 1978. $20.00 – 25.00.

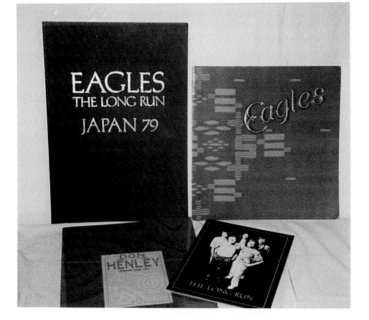

Left to right: Eagles '79 Japan, very rare, $25.00 – 60.00 or more. Eagles '76 US tour book, $10.00 – 25.00. Don Henley '91 tour book, $10.00 – 20.00. Eagles '79 US tour book, $10.00 – 25.00.

Heart, "bébé le strange" tour program, 1980. $20.00 – 25.00.

George Harrison's only U.S. tour, 1974. $30.00 – 40.00.

Heart, tour programs from various concerts. $20.00 – 25.00 each.

Michael Jackson, tour programs from various concerts, $25.00 – 40.00 each.

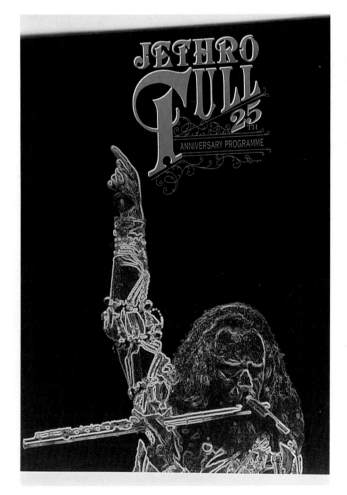

Jethro Tull, "25th Anniversary" tour program. $15.00 – 20.00.

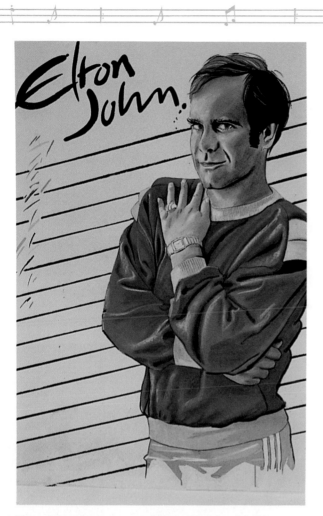

Elton John, tour program, 1980, $15.00 – 20.00.

Elton John, "Rock of the Westies" tour program, 1975, $20.00 – 30.00.

Journey, tour program, 1980, $15.00 – 20.00.

KISS, tour programs from various concerts. Programs before 1980, $40.00 – 60.00. Programs after 1981, $20.00 – 25.00.

The Monkees, tour program, 1967. $35.00 – 45.00.

Madonna, tour programs, $25.00 – 40.00 each. Far right, "Virgin Tour," $50.00 – 125.00.

Paul McCartney, tour program, 1989/90. $15.00 – 25.00.

Paul McCartney, press kit, 1989/90. $50.00 – 75.00.

The Moody Blues, "The Present" tour program, 1983. $15.00 – 20.00.

The Moody Blues, "Long Distance Voyager" tour program, 1987. $15.00 – 20.00.

The Moody Blues, tour program, 1978. $15.00 – 20.00.

Ted Nugent, tour program, 1979/80. $15.00 – 20.00.

Ringo Starr, tour program 1989/90. $15.00 – 20.00.

Beatles concert tickets, 1964 – 1966, unused tickets. $200.00 – 400.00.

Beatles, concert tickets, 1964 – 1965. Values same as page 198.

Beatles, concert ticket, September 3, 1964, Indiana State Fair, unused. $300.00 – 400.00.

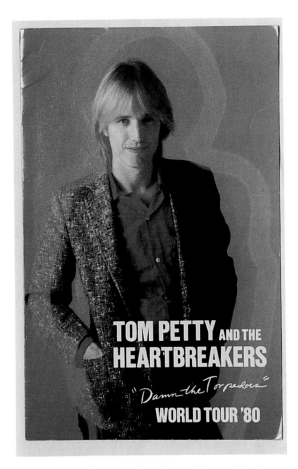

Tom Petty & The Heartbreakers, "Damn the Torpedoes" tour program, 1980. $20.00 – 30.00.

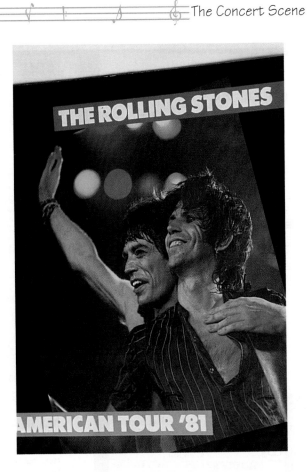

The Rolling Stones, tour program, 1981. $20.00 – 30.00.

Wings, Japan tour program. This was for a tour that never happened, 1980. $85.00 – 100.00.

Wings, "Over America" tour program, 1976. $30.00 – 40.00.

Beatles, concert tickets, 1966. See page 198.

Beatles, concert tickets, 1966. (Note: tickets from Suffolk Downs, Boston, Mass., are quite easy to find and are valued in the $35.00 – 75.00 range.)

Beatles, concert ticket, Aug. 16, 1966, John F. Kennedy Stadium, Phila., PA, unused. $300.00 – 400.00.

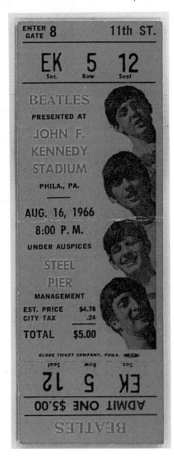

Concert tickets, various artists, 1974 – current. $10.00 – 20.00 each.

Concert tickets, various artists, 1974 – current. $10.00 – 20.00 each.

Backstage passes, various artists.
$10.00 – 30.00 each.

Concert tickets and backstage passes, various artists.
$10.00 – 30.00 each.

Instruments

Some performers' actual stage instruments are featured in this chapter. These instruments demand high dollar at auctions across the world. Most one-of-a-kind instruments, like the ones featured, are in personal collections around the globe. Similar in nature are instruments featured in museums around the world, such as the Rock-n-Roll Hall of Fame or the Smithsonian. The Buddy Holly guitar featured in this book was bought and used by Buddy himself. He purchased this Gibson J-45 in the 1940s and owned the guitar at the time of his death. Buddy composed a lot of songs on this special guitar; this rock-n-roll treasure is currently valued at over $300,000.

With the dawn of the rock-n-roll guitar star in the mid 1950s came the advent of the toy guitar. Toy manufacturers began production of officially licensed merchandise so the pre-teen audience could pretend to be like their favorite hero. In 1956, the first toy guitar to feature a rock-n-roll

artist was created and produced by Elvis Presley Enterprises. Toy instruments quickly became a popular item with toy manufacturers shortly thereafter, most notably The Beatles officially licensed toy instruments created by Mastro Industries in the USA and Selcol in the UK from 1964 – 1966.

Tambourines, harmonicas, drum sets, bongos, banjos, and many guitars were created for all our favorite rock-n-roll heroes. The guitars varied from ukulele-size to full-size instruments. All toy instruments produced were meant to be played, another factor contributing to their rarity. All these instruments are considered valuable in today's market place and since production was limited, toy instruments are scarce.

Blue Oyster Cult, signed guitar, 1989. $1,000.00 – 1,500.00.

Bob Dylan played this Fender Tele-
caster at the Bill Clinton Inaugur-
al Ball, 1992. He played with
Stephen Stills during the show.
$5,000.00 – 6,000.00.

Bob Dylan guitar, 1980s. Signed on back of headstock. $6,000.00 – 8,000.00.

Jimi Hendrix, mixing board from the Electric Lady Studio A in N.Y.C., 1970. Jimi used this to record his "Cry of Love" LP. $20,000.00 – 25,000.00.

Pearl Jam, guitar, signed by the band, $2,000.00 – 2,500.00.

Rickenbacker, guitar, signed by Tom Petty, 2-6-90. $900.00 – 1,200.00.

A mid-1940s Gibson J-45 guitar purchased by Buddy Holly and owned by Buddy until his death. The custom leatherwork was done by Buddy himself. One of Buddy's favorite guitars. $250,000.00 – 300,000.00.

Stevie Ray Vaughan and Jeff Beck signed this guitar during their 1989 tour. $2,000.00 – 2,500.00.

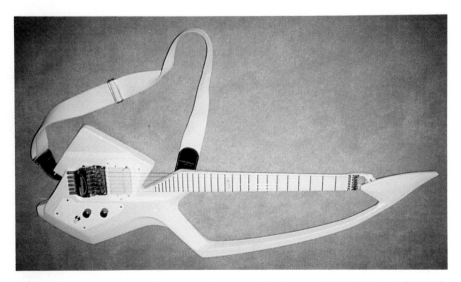

Prince's white cloud guitar, late 1980s, owned and used by Prince. $7,000.00 – 10,000.00.

Steve Vai signed guitar, early 1990s, $700.00 – 900.00.

Eddie Van Halen owned and played this, handmade guitar. Built by him in 1986. It was featured in *Guitar World Magazine* in an article about how he builds guitars. Raffled off by NAMM (National Association of Music Merchandisers) in 1987. $15,000.00 – 20,000.00.

Guitar, 1964, mfg. by Mastro Industries, US, pink plastic with lapel clip on back, rubber bands as strings, Beatles pictured. $175.00 – 200.00. A cardboard store display titled "Beatles Pin-Up Guitar" held 12 of these guitar pins. See Mastro Catalog 1966 advertisement for picture of this display. Very rare, $2,000.00 – 4,000.00.

Guitar, 1964, manufactured by Mastro Industries, US, 15", 4-string "Jr. Guitar" on original cardboard backing with instruction sheet. Loose, $600.00 – 900.00. Carded, $1,200.00 – 1,800.00. Promotional version was made with Beatles' faces printed over a white background, see "Yeah Yeah Guitar" for reference. Loose, $2,000.00 – 4,000.00. Carded, $3,000.00 – 5,000.00. Color variations are common on promotional guitars.

Guitar, 1964, manufactured by Mastro Industries, US, 21", pink and red. "Four Pop Guitar" sealed on original cardboard backing with instruction sheet, 4-string. Loose, $750.00 – 1,000.00. Carded, $1,500.00 – 2,000.00. Promotional version, Beatles' faces printed over white background. Loose, $2,500.00 – 5,000.00. Carded, $4,000.00 – 7,000.00.

Guitar, 1964, manufactured by Mastro Industries, US, 30", maroon and pink "Beatle-ist Guitar," 6 strings. Loose, $1,000.00 – 1,500.00. Carded, $2,000.00 – 3,000.00 with instruction sheet. Promotional version, loose, $4,000.00 – 6,000.00. Carded, $6,000.00 – 8,000.00.

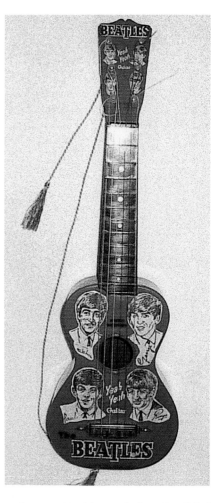

Banjo, 1964, manufactured by Mastro Industries, US, 22", maroon, gold, and red, white face with Beatles pictured in red, 4 colored strings, maroon bridge and Beatles pictured on headstock. Loose, $4,000.00 – 6,000.00. Carded, $6,000.00 – 10,000.00.

Guitar, 1964, manufactured by Mastro Industries, US, 23", 6 strings, maroon and red "Yeah Yeah Guitar." This guitar is the rarest of all the Mastro and Selcol stringed instruments. Loose, $5,000.00 – 7,000.00. Carded, $8,000.00 – 11,000,00. Promotional version, Beatles' faces printed over a white background. Loose $7,000.00 – 10,000. Carded, $11,000.00 – 14,000.00.

Bongos, 1964, manufactured by Mastro Industries, US, "Beat Bongos," 5¼" high, red and maroon with group stickers, white skins. Loose, $5,000.00 – 8,000.00. Boxed, $8,000.00 – 12,000.00. Also came in slightly larger "Big Beat Bongos," 6½" high, red and black with group stickers, priced the same.

Drum, 1964, manufactured by Mastro Industries, US, 14", red and gold, Beatles' faces and autographs on skin. Drum only, $2,000.00 – 3,000.00. Boxed with sticks, stand and instructions, $4,000.00 – 6,000.00.

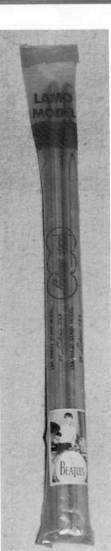

Guitars and banjo, all the stringed instruments manufactured by Mastro Industries, US, 1964. See individual items for values.

Drumsticks, 1964, manufactured by Ludwig, US, pair of wooden sticks states "Ringo Starr Model" on each, in original packaging with b/w photo card of Ringo. In package, $750.00 – 1,200.00. Loose, $250.00 – 500.00.

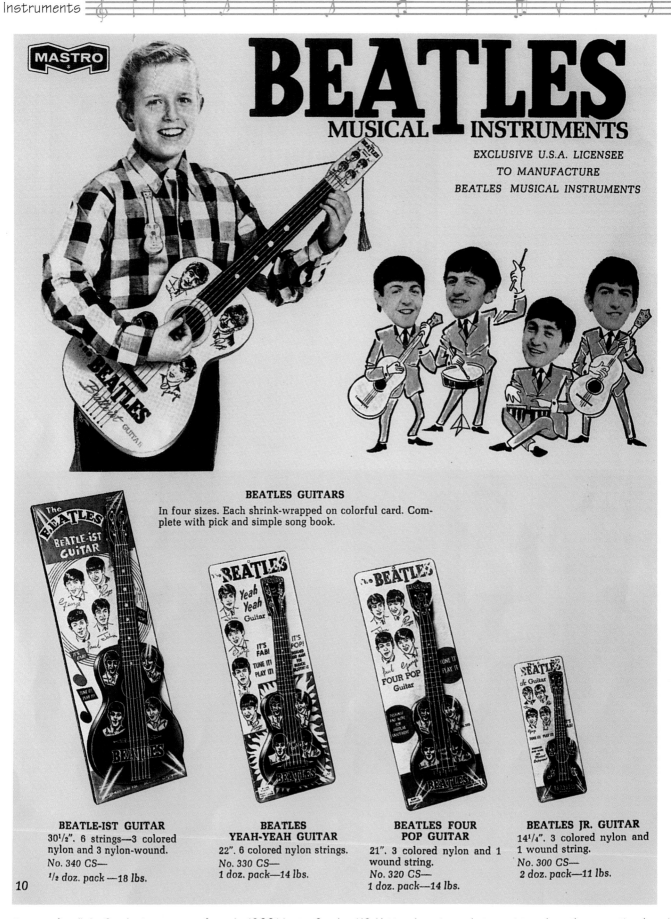

MASTRO

BEATLES
MUSICAL INSTRUMENTS

EXCLUSIVE U.S.A. LICENSEE
TO MANUFACTURE
BEATLES MUSICAL INSTRUMENTS

BEATLES GUITARS

In four sizes. Each shrink-wrapped on colorful card. Complete with pick and simple song book.

BEATLE-IST GUITAR
30½". 6 strings—3 colored
nylon and 3 nylon-wound.
No. 340 CS—
½ doz. pack —18 lbs.

**BEATLES
YEAH-YEAH GUITAR**
22". 6 colored nylon strings.
No. 330 CS—
1 doz. pack—14 lbs.

**BEATLES FOUR
POP GUITAR**
21". 3 colored nylon and 1
wound string.
No. 320 CS—
1 doz. pack—14 lbs.

BEATLES JR. GUITAR
14¼". 3 colored nylon and
1 wound string.
No. 300 CS—
2 doz. pack—11 lbs.

10

Advertisement for all the Beatles instruments from the 1966 Mastro Catalog, US. Notice the guitars that are pictured are the promotional versions.

212

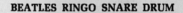

BEATLES BANJO

Full-size 22" banjo-uke with perfect pitch. Accurately fretted fingerboard has engraved position marks. Weatherproof head. Tension rods. Patented tuning keys. Pick and song book. On shrink-wrapped colorful card.

No. 350 CS—$^1/_2$ doz. pack—13 lbs.

BEATLES BONGOS

Weatherproof head . . . always in tune. Permanently stretched for maximum resonance and quick response. Non-slip foam discs on sides. Simple-to-follow instruction booklet. In eye-appealing display merchandiser.

No. 360 PDB—
BEAT BONGO
(Height 5$^1/_4$", heads 5" and 5$^3/_4$"), $^1/_2$ doz. pack— 10 lbs.

No. 370 PDB—
BIG BEAT BONGO
(Height 6$^1/_4$", Heads 6$^1/_4$" and 7$^1/_4$") $^1/_2$ doz. pack—15 lbs.

BEATLES RINGO SNARE DRUM

Full size, 14" x 6$^1/_2$", snare drum with brilliant tone quality and deep resonance. Golden hoop and attachments, red, gold-sparkled shell. Adjustable tension rods. On and off snare mechanism. Abrased batterhead for brush effects. Adjustable steel tripod stand. Balanced wood drum sticks. Simple instruction booklet. Packaged in colorful portable case.

No. 380 PCC—$^1/_4$ doz. pack—21 lbs.

MASTRO BEATLES "PIN-UP" GUITAR

Miniature of the popular Mastro Beatles playing guitars. Only 5" with built-in clip. Beatles' likenesses printed on face.

No. P3-DB—
DISPLAY BOX
2 dozen guitars in box.
Packed 6 boxes to carton. 6 lbs.

No. P3-DC—
DISPLAY CARD
1 dozen guitars to a card.
Packed 1 dozen cards to carton. 6 lbs.

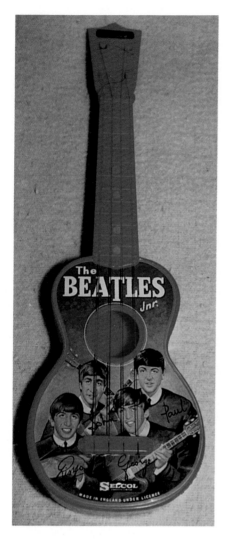

Guitar, 1964, manufactured by Selcol, UK, 32", red orange and maroon "New Beat Guitar," 4 strings. Loose, $600.00 – 800.00. Boxed, $1,000.00 – 1,200.00.

Guitar, 1964, manufactured by Selcol, UK, 14", orange 4-string with color paper photo of the Beatles, "Jnr. Guitar." Loose, $3,500.00 – 4,500.00. Carded, $5,000.00 – 6,000.00.

Another guitar has 6 strings and is called the "Big 6 Guitar." Valued the same as the New Beat Guitar above.

Guitar, 1964, manufactured by Selcol, UK, 21" 4-string, "Big Beat Guitar," orange and cream or all orange. Loose, $2,000.00 – 2,500.00. Boxed, $3,000.00 – 4,000.00.

Guitar, 1964, manufactured by Selcol, UK, 23" 4-string "New Sound Guitar." Loose, $750.00 – 1,000.00. Carded, $2,000.00 – 3,500.00.

Guitar, 1964, manufactured by Selcol, UK, 30" 4-string "Cut-Away Guitar," orange and maroon. Loose, $1,500.00 – 2,000.00. No backing card or box known to exist.

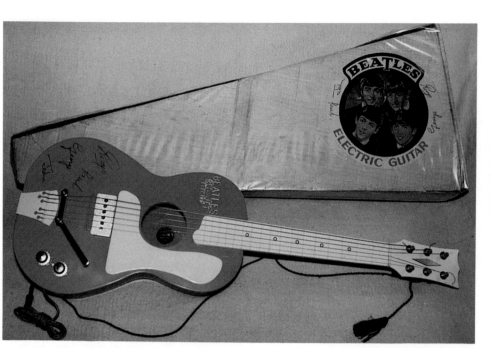

Guitar, 1964, manufactured by Selcol, UK, 31" 6-string "Red Jet Electric Guitar," orange and cream. Loose, $2,500.00 – 3,500.00. Boxed, $3,500.00 – 4,500.00.

Drum, 1964, manufactured by Selcol, UK, 14", "New Beat Drum," maroon and orange, Ringo Starr autograph and picture on skin. Loose with stand, $800.00 – 1,100.00. Boxed, $1,800.00 – 2,200.00. A third variation exists which has no picture of Ringo on drumskin. Valued the same as this version.

Drum, 1964, manufactured by Selcol, UK, 14", "Ringo Starr Drum," gold and red, large picture of Ringo Starr on skin, sold with cymbal, stand, and sticks. Loose, $1,000.00 – 1,200.00. Boxed, $2,000.00 – 2,500.00.

The Monkees, very rare drum set from 1967, US. $1,000.00 – 1,500.00.

The Bee Gees, toy guitar, US. $175.00 – 200.00

Donnie and Marie, US, 1970s. $35.00 – 65.00.

"The Monkees," 1967, Raybert Productions, tambourine. Loose, $85.00 – 125.00. Boxed, $200.00 – 250.00.

The Monkees, plastic 14" wind-up guitar by Mattel, 1966, US. $125.00 – 150.00.

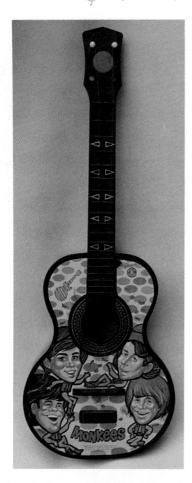

The Monkees, plastic 20" toy guitar by Mattel, 1966, US. $175.00 – 200.00.

The Monkees, rare plastic toy guitar by Lapin, 1968, US. $600.00 – 700.00.

The Rolling Stones, UK, 1964, manufactured by Selcol, rare 32" guitar. $800.00 – 1,200.00.

KISS, guitar by Carnival Toys, 1977. $250.00 – 300.00.

KISS, drum set, owned by Peter Criss, mid-1970s, $2,500.00 – 3,500.00.

Autographs

One of the fastest growing fields of collecting today has become the area of rock-n-roll autographs. We present a multitude of rare examples in our book. Nearly every major rock-n-roll artist since the 1950s is represented. Probably the 'crème de la crème' in this field is the Beatles. Obtaining a legitimate set of all four Beatles autographs has become increasingly difficult, to say nothing of the rising cost of such a set as they continue to increase in value.

The most important factor in determining value of an authentic signed piece lies with what the autograph was signed on, in increasing order of importance: a blank piece of paper, a fan club card or photograph signed on the back, an official/legal document, a handwritten letter, a record jacket, and finally a photograph signed on the front. Beyond these, handwritten lyrics to published songs have become the pinnacle of rock-n-roll collecting. Several prime examples of original Beatles handwritten lyrics have sold in the $100,000 to over $240,000 range in recent years. We have included a superb example of Beatles handwritten lyrics for this chapter. For the first time in print anywhere is "You've Got To Hide Your Love Away" written in 1965 by John Lennon. This is considered to be a first draft of this popular Beatles song. A first draft is definitely more valuable than a rewrite in the field of handwritten lyrics. Rewrites of lyrics are important and very rare but are not as valuable or desir-

able as first drafts. First drafts reflect the moment in time when the initial inspiration for a song came and were usually written on whatever the artist had available at the time, i.e., notepaper, envelopes, hotel stationery, even matchbook covers. A first draft might contain some cross-outs and notes the artist made at the time. Some words might be different than the final song lyrics. A first draft might only contain important pieces of the song such as the chorus or an opening verse or two and not necessarily the entire song. These are usually good indications of a first draft. Rewrites of lyrics were commonly done to take to the recording studio so others involved could read them. These rewrites are usually found on standard paper, and the lyrics typically reflect the final published version of the song.

Please note that the buyer must exercise extreme caution in collecting autographs. Research before buying is very important: this is absolutely necessary! This field, like others, has been plagued with many clever forgeries over the years. Fortunately there are handwriting experts who specialize in legitimate signed artifacts. It is the buyers' responsibility to make sure they deal with reputable dealers that are experts in their field. Many such experts have narrowed their expertise to just a few or one particular rock-n-roll artist. Be sure before buying your dealer is an expert in the area you are interested in.

AC/DC, post-Bon Scott era.
$80.00 – 100.00.

Aerosmith, autographed LP cover. $80.00 –
100.00.

The Allman Brothers Band, original line-up with
Duane Allman. Value depends on condition, etc.
Duane Allman's autograph is very rare. $500.00 –
800.00.

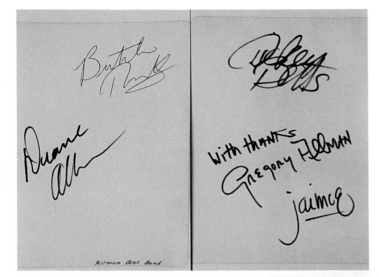

The Allman Brothers Band, original line-up again (minus bassist Berry Oakley). $300.00 – 500.00.

The Animals with their 1966 line-up. $150.00 – 175.00.

Bachman-Turner Overdrive, signed L.P. $50.00 – 70.00.

Bad Company original four members, signed L.P. $75.00 – 85.00.

Badfinger autographs. This band is notorious for signing items with their first names only (especially Mike Gibbins). Finding an item signed by two of the four with first names is most common. On paper, $400.00 – 500.00. On photo, $600.00 – 750.00. On L.P. cover, $500.00 – 600.00.

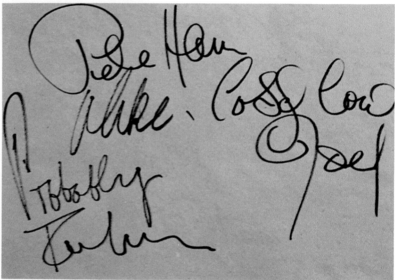

Beach Boys, signed L.P., post-Brian Wilson line-up, 1965 – late 1970s. $110.00 – 125.00.

		WITH JOHN
1	Hallelujah.	Cathy's Clown
2	That's Alright Mama. ✳	✳ One after 9.09.
3	Stuck On you.	✳ Words of love.
4	Tutti Frutti.	✳ I'll never let you go.
5	Long Tall Sally.	✳ I wonder if I care as much
6	What did I say?	✳ Sure to fall.
7	Red Sails in the Sunset.	FOR JOHN TO TRY
8	Whole Lotta Shakin'.	✳ Alright OK you win.
9	Mean Woman blues.	
10	I don't care if the sun don't shine. ✳	
11	Honey Don't.	
12	Clarabella. ✳	

POSSIBLES..?
1 Rip it up.
2 Fabulous.
3 Lotta Lovin.
4 Kansas City.
5 Jenny, Jenny.

13 Little Queenie. ✳

Oh my soul
Lucille

Words
Strings
Plec.

✳ ones which aren't done every week.

GROSVENOR

This is the earliest Beatles set list known to exist. Written by a 17-year-old Paul McCartney for a show The Silver Beetles did on June 4, 1960, at the Grosvenor Ballroom in Wallasey. There is only one Lennon/McCartney original on this list, "One After 909," all other songs were covers of their influences, Elvis, Little Richard, Buddy Holly, the Everly Brothers, Ray Charles, Carl Perkins, etc. $40,000.00 – 60,000.00.

THE SHOREHAM — WASHINGTON, D.C.

① Beethoven
② From me to You.
③ I saw her standing there.
④ This Boy.
⑤ All my loving,
⑥ I wanna be your man.
⑦ Please Please Me.
⑧ Til there was you.
⑨ She loves you,
⑩ I want to Hold your Hand.
⑪ Twist and Shout
⑫ Long tail Sally.

Set list from the Beatles' first-ever American concert, Washington Coliseum, Washington, D.C., on Tuesday, February 11, 1964. Written by John Lennon in their suite at the Shoreham Hotel. $50,000.00 – 75,000.00.

224

Beatles, signed autograph book page, 1963.
$3,000.00 – 3,500.00.

Beatles autographs, circa 1963 –
1964. $3,000.00 – 3,500.00.

Beatles, signed 45 picture sleeve, January 1964.
$7,000.00 – 9,000.00.

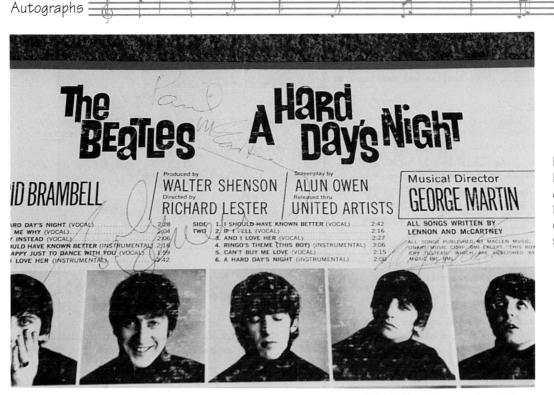

Beatles, signed authentic LP covers, very rare. This one only John, Paul, and Ringo signed on the back. George signed on the front! $4,500.00 – 5,500.00.

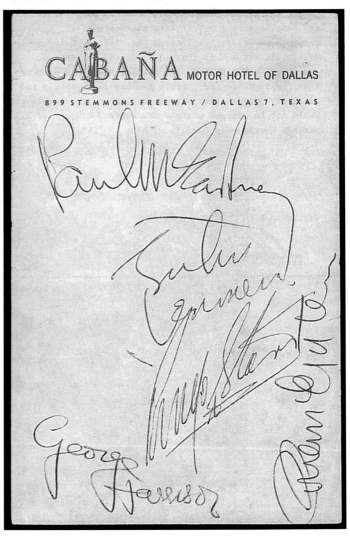

Autographs of The Beatles and manager Brian Epstein on stationery from the Cabana Hotel in Dallas. Signed for the Dallas Fan Club president, Stephanie Pinter, September 18, 1964. $4,000.00 – 6,000.00.

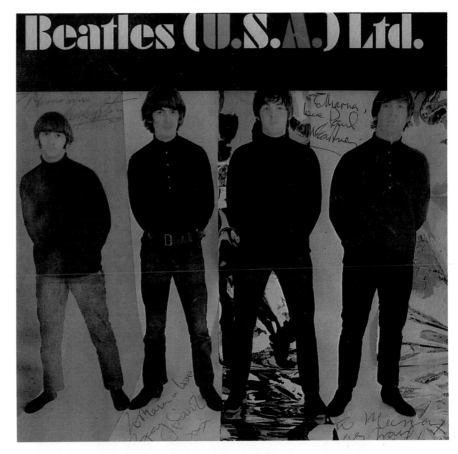

Beatles, a signed 1966 American Tour Program, featuring a great full-color photograph of the Beatles on the cover. This piece was signed August 11, 1966, on a flight between London and Boston, the same day John Lennon apologized to the world for his remarks about Christianity. 1966 sets are very hard to find, and signed color photographs of the Beatles are nearly impossible to find. $12,000.00 – 15,000.00.

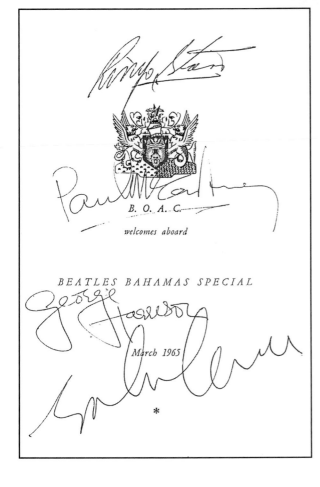

The Beatles' autographs on a BOAC flight menu entitled "The Beatles Bahamas Special." Signed March 10, 1965, on the flight leaving the Bahamas after filming sequences for their second film, "Help!" $5,000.00 – 7,000.00.

Beatles, signed inside cover of program of their December 1965 final tour of Britain. $6,000.00 – 7,500.00.

Beatles, signed 8" x 10" photo, all four signatures, mid-1964. Signed photographs of this type are rare. $6,500.00 – 8,000.00.

One of the last autographs ever given by John Lennnon on his "Double Fantasy" L.P. $3,000.00 – 4,000.00.

Beatles, another 1964 example.
$3,000.00 – 3,500.00.

237

THE BEATLES

The Beatles' autographs signed on the title page of the famous Hunter Davies biography. Signed in the summer of 1969 on the steps of the EMI Abbey Road Studios during the recording of the "Abbey Road" album. Signed in-person for American Apple Scruff Carol Bedford. (1969 autograph sets are extremely rare!) $5,000.00 – 7,000.00.

Beatles, John Lennon signed the back of this "Magical Mystery" Tour English EP, 1967, $1,000.00 – 1,500.00.

Beatles, bank check signed by Ringo Starr, October 29, 1970. $500.00 – 600.00.

Beatles, bank check signed by George Harrison, June 4, 1971. $600.00 – 700.00.

Beatles, bank check signed by John Lennon, June 16, 1971. $1,200.00 – 1,400.00.

Bee Gees, the original five-member line-up. Very rare, early group. $125.00 – 200.00.

Big Brother & The Holding Company. This piece features just Janis Joplin and one band member, Peter Albin. Janis Joplin's signature can be worth $500.00 – 1,000.00, depending on the piece.

Black Sabbath, original four members, including Ozzy Osborne. $150.00 – 200.00.

David Bowie. $70.00 – 100.00.

The Byrds, original five members.
$175.00 – 250.00.

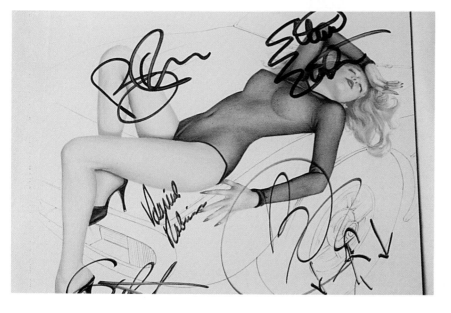

The Cars. $60.00 – 75.00.

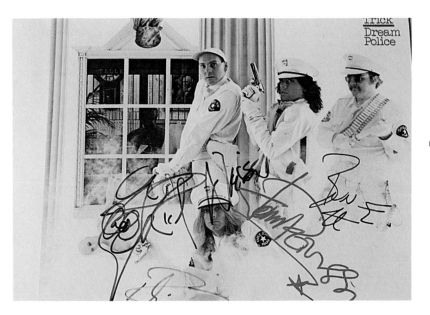

Cheap Trick. $50.00 – 60.00.

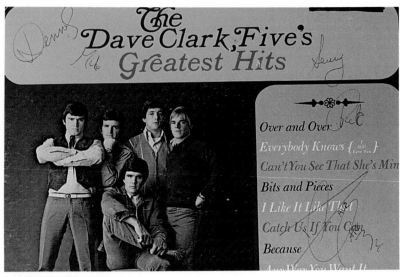

The Dave Clark Five. $175.00 – 250.00.

Joe Cocker with Chris Stainton. $60.00 – 80.00.

Creedence Clearwater Revival, all four original members. $250.00 – 350.00.

Cream, piece includes all three members. $200.00 – 350.00.

Crosby, Stills, Nash & Young. $180.00 – 200.00.

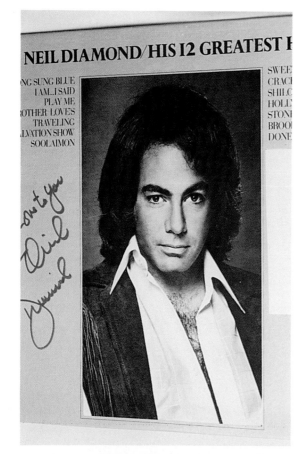

Neil Diamond. $95.00 – 120.00.

Fats Domino. $60.00 – 80.00.

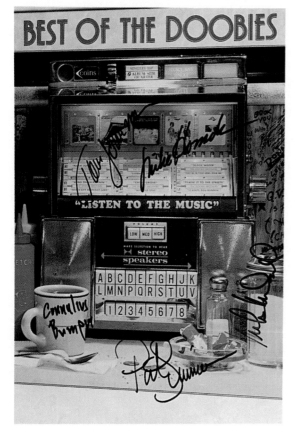

The Doobie Brothers. $75.00 – 95.00.

The Easybeats, quite rare and unique. $150.00 – 200.00.

Fabian. $30.00 – 40.00.

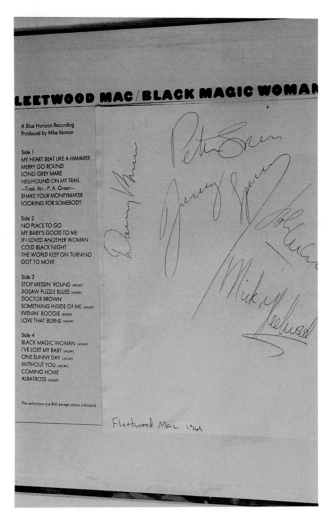

Fleetwood Mac, original five member line-up. $350.00 – 700.00.

Heart, Ann & Nancy Wilson. $40.00 – 50.00.

The Jimi Hendrix Experience. Values can be higher depending on the items signed. $800.00 – 1,500.00.

The Hollies, original line-up. $175.00 – 250.00.

Michael Jackson. $150.00 – 250.00.

Jefferson Airplane, all six members, 1967. $100.00 – 150.00.

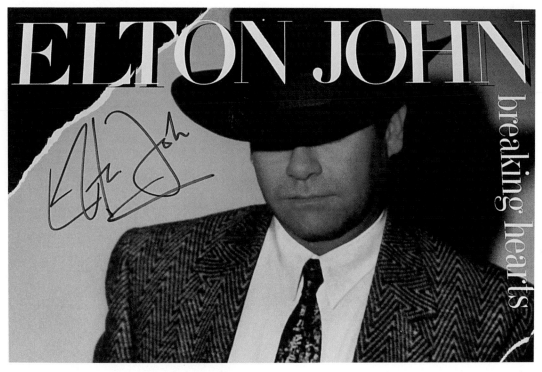

Elton John. $60.00 – 85.00.

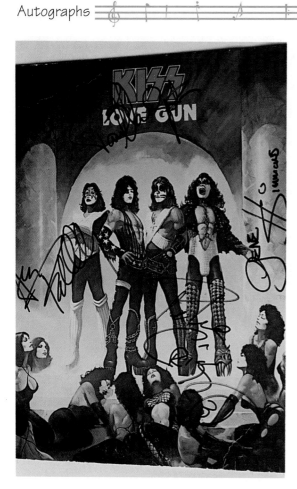

KISS, original line-up. $100.00 – 200.00.

Led Zeppelin. $300.00 – 600.00.

The Lovin' Spoonful, 1966. $100.00 – 125.00.

Lynyrd Skynyrd, 1976 – 1977, the last line-up of the group before the fatal plane crash. $400.00 – 500.00.

The Monkees original pilot script from 1965, signed by all four Monkees in 1997. This is number 23, the script that was the audition for the TV show when many people such as Stephen Stills and Paul Williams auditioned. $600.00 – 900.00.

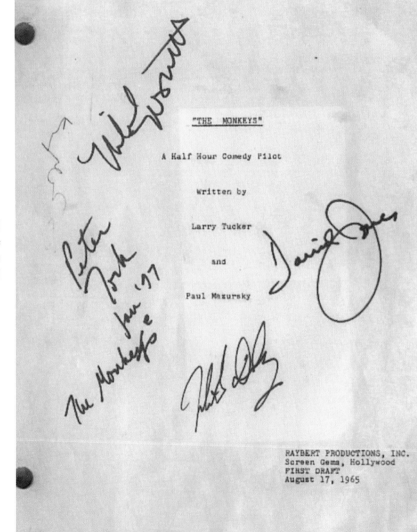

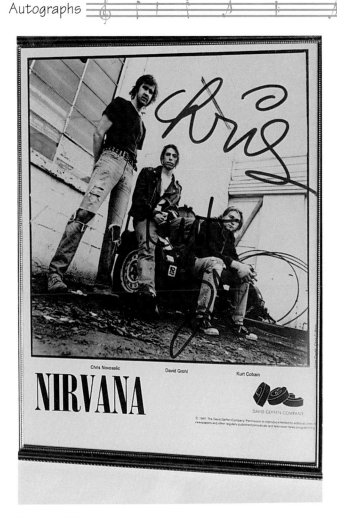

Nirvana. $200.00 – 400.00.

The very best of ROY ORBISON

The songs in this album represent a high plateau in the career of Roy Orbison—a period or era which I am going to call his "Monument Period." It is this period and the associations thereof which, I think, crystallized the talents latent in Roy. It was during this time that he had a truly remarkable string of hits—at a time when real hits seemed exceedingly difficult to come by. It was during this era that Roy really developed into a genuine "name" singer—at a time

when "one shot artists" were the rule rather than the exception.

I wish the greatest of success to Roy in all his future endeavors and I feel that he has the ability to accomplish many great triumphs. At the same time, I must say that no matter what success may come his way, Roy Orbison's "Monument Period" will always represent one of his topmost pinnacles of achievement and one of the great contributions to the world of popular music.

BOUDLEAUX BRYANT

Side one
ONLY THE LONELY
(Orbison-Melson) Acuff Rose Pub. BMI 2:24
CRYING
(Orbison-Melson) Acuff Rose Pub. BMI 2:45
RUNNING SCARED
(Orbison-Melson) Acuff Rose Pub. BMI 2:10
IT'S OVER
(Orbison-Dees) Acuff Rose Pub. BMI 2:47
CANDY MAN
(Ross-Neil) January Music BMI 2:48

Side two
OH PRETTY WOMAN
(Orbison-Dees) Acuff Rose Pub. BMI 2:55
BLUE ANGEL
(Orbison-Melson) Acuff Rose Pub. BMI 2:50
IN DREAMS
(Orbison) Acuff Rose Pub. BMI 2:46
DREAM BABY
(Cindy Walker) Combine Music BMI 2:35
MEAN WOMAN BLUES
(C. DeMetrius) Gladys Music ASCAP 2:23

Fred Foster, Producer. Bill Porter, Engineer. Tommy Strong, Technician.

MLP 8045
SLP 18045   5   A Full Frequency High Fidelity Recording

monument is artistry

Roy Orbison. $125.00 – 250.00.

Pink Floyd. $250.00 – 350.00.

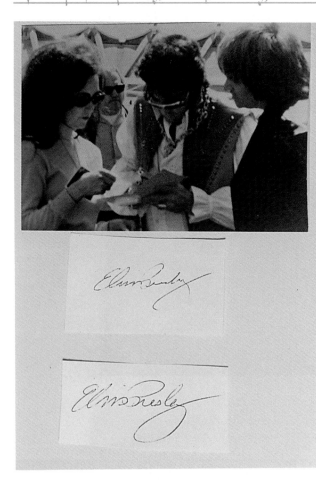

Billy Preston. $35.00 – 50.00.

Elvis Presley. His memorabilia ranks with that of the Beatles and commands the widest value range among rock-n-roll celebrities. $300.00 – 800.00.

Queen, very collectible group since Freddie Mercury's death. $250.00 – 500.00.

The Righteous Brothers. $50.00 – 65.00.

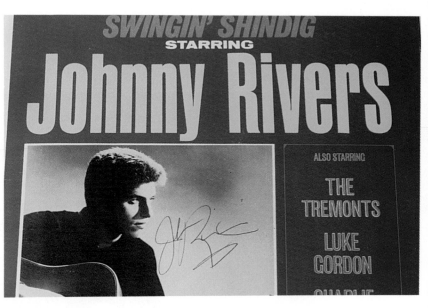

Johnny Rivers. $30.00 – 40.00.

Rolling Stones original lineup, 1966. In-person signed photos as this can easily fetch $600.00 – 1,000.00!

Todd Rundgren. $40.00 – 60.00.

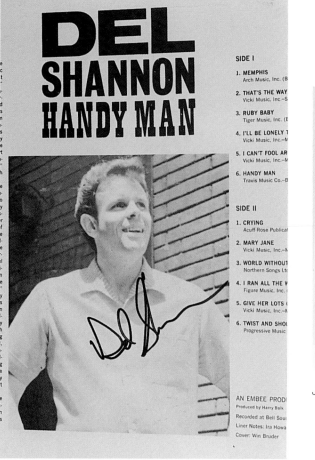

Johnnie Ray. $50.00 – 85.00.

Del Shannon. As is the case with artists who are now deceased, the cost is generally higher than others of the same era. $90.00 – 125.00.

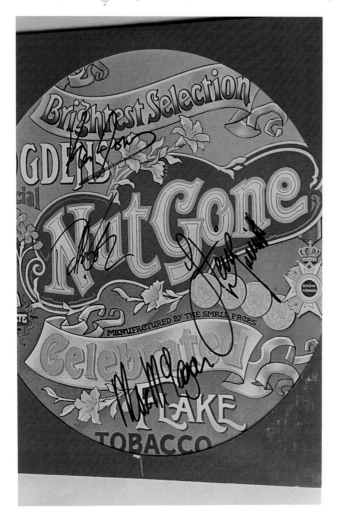

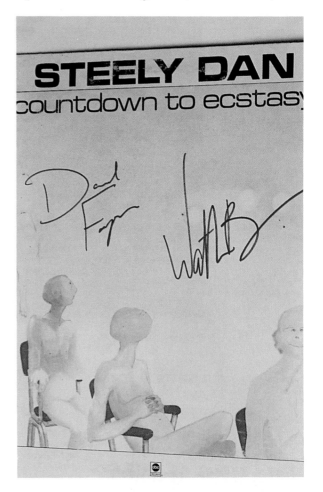

Small Faces. $175.00 – 300.00. A piece such as this can easily fetch higher dollars in auctions.

Steely Dan, the two lead members, Donald Fagen and Walter Becker. $75.00 – 100.00.

Rod Stewart, piece includes several band members including Carmine Appice. $90.00 – 120.00.

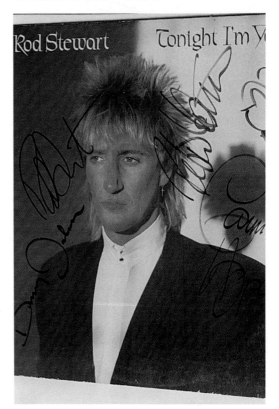

The Talking Heads. $85.00 – 100.00.

James Taylor. $60.00 – 70.00.

The Turtles, original six man line-up.
1966. $150.00 – 175.00.

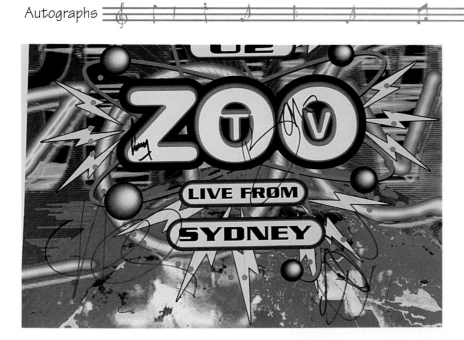

U2. $200.00 – 375.00. Current groups like this can be very valuable.

The Who original line-up, $300.00 – 500.00. Prices can easily rise if Keith Moon has signed.

Jackie Wilson, somewhat difficult autograph to obtain. $95.00 – 175.00.

The Yardbirds, vintage signed photograph.
$250.00 – 300.00.

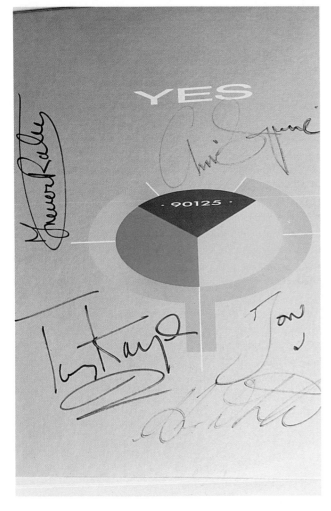

Yes, later line-up. $70.00 – 80.00.

Frank Zappa. $200.00 – 300.00.

Cartoon Groups

Yellow Submarine

"We all live in a Yellow Submarine"… Surely everyone, young and old, recognizes this line from one of the Beatles' most famous songs. This full-length feature movie, which premiered in London in July of 1968, represented a technological breakthrough for the movie industry of the 1960s. Real life imagery integrated with animated artistry plus the addition of Beatles music made this film a classic for all time. The film coincided with the psychedelic era of the 1960s and with its vivid colors coupled with its good vs. evil theme remains a constant reminder to us of the Sixties.

The Yellow Submarine artistry was the brainchild of German artist Heinz Edelmann, not American artist Peter Max as many believe. His remarkable talents are evident in his creative interpretations of each Beatle and the multitude of characters he created for the film.

The Yellow Submarine represented the second rush of Beatles merchandising efforts in late 1968. Following a very successful 1964 – 1966 merchandising campaign, NEMS Enterprises Ltd. in conjunction with SUBA Films Ltd. pro-

duced a plethora of licensed merchandise ranging from simple items like childrens lunchboxes and toys to more limited production items like in-store promotional displays, original art animation production cells used in the movie, and hand-painted figurine sets by the world-renowned Goebel Corporation of West Germany.

These artifacts have since become very prized collectibles. The movie lends itself perfectly to a merchandising effort: seemingly limitless items could be manufactured utilizing extremely colorful vivid scenery from the film. Many licensees produced official Yellow Submarine memorabilia from late 1968 throughout 1969. Many of these products have been cataloged but there are still collectors today that uncover previously unknown licensed pieces. Many collectors have begun concentrating on Yellow Submarine merchandise, favoring it over earlier Beatles memorabilia because of its vibrant, eye-catching appeal and the wide variety of products produced.

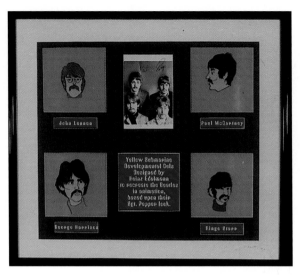

Art Animation, 1968, early developmental cels created by Heinz Edelmann. $4,000.00 – 5,000.00 set.

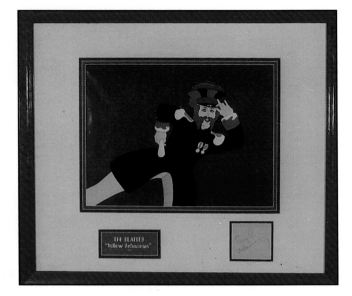

Art Animation, 1968, UK, King Features, production art cel of Paul McCartney from the Yellow Submarine movie. $3,000.00 – 3,500.00.

Art Animation, 1968, UK, King Features, production art cel of John Lennon from the Yellow Submarine movie. $2,500.00 – 3,000.00.

Art Animation, 1968, UK, King Features, production art cel from the Yellow Submarine movie of a Blue Meanie and Bulldogs. $2,000.00 – 2,500.00.

Art Animation, 1968, UK, King Features, production art cell from the Yellow Submarine movie, each 6-8" tall. Paul, $1,000.00 – 1,500.00; Ringo, $1,200.00 – 1,500.00; George, $1,000.00 – 1,500.00; John, $1,200.00 – 1,500.00.

Art Animation, 1968, UK, King Features, production art cels from the Yellow Submarine movie, large Ringo, $3,000.00 – 4,000.00; whale, $400.00 – 500.00. The Ringo cel is a 4-sheet overlay; his head, eyes, and mouth are on separate celluloid sheets. From the "Nowhere Man" sequence.

Art Animation, 1968, UK, King Features, production art cels from the Yellow Submarine movie, Bulldog in piano, $1,500.00 – 2,000.00; the Boob, $200.00 – 250.00; Mini Blue Meanie with Bulldogs on leash, $700.00 – 1,000.00.

Art Animation, 1968, UK, King Features, production art cels from the Yellow Submarine movie. The Flying Glove, $1,200.00 – 1,500.00; Head Blue Meanie, $800.00 – 1,000.00; Butterfly Stomper, $400.00 – 500.00.

Art Animation, 1968, UK, King Features, production art cels from the Yellow Submarine movie. Blue Meanie, $500.00 – 700.00; Paul, $1,000.00 – 1,200.00; Stone People, $100.00 – 150.00.

Art Animation, 1968, UK, King Features, production art cels from the Yellow Submarine movie, 6-9" tall. $1,200.00 – 1,500.00 each.

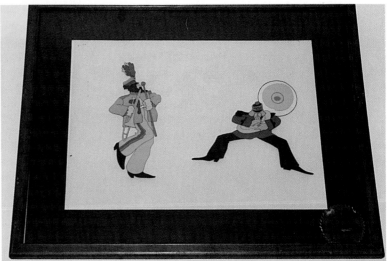

Art Animation, 1968, UK, King Features, production art cels from the Yellow Submarine movie. The Yellow Submarine, rare, $1,500.00 – 2,000.00; whale, $400.00 – 500.00. Art cels of the submarine itself are difficult to find handpainted. King Features used decals of the submarine throughout the film instead of hand painting a cel each time the sub was used.

Art Animation, 1968, UK, King Features, Certificate of Authenticity which accompanied each Yellow Submarine art cel sold. $100.00 – 125.00.

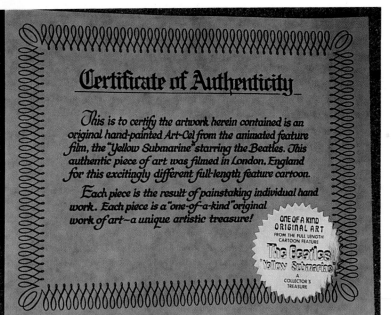

Art Animation, 1968, UK, King Features, pre-production drawings, Bulldog sequence, scenes 26 & 27 from the Yellow Submarine movie. $800.00 – 1,000.00 set of three. See next page for scene 28, third in the set.

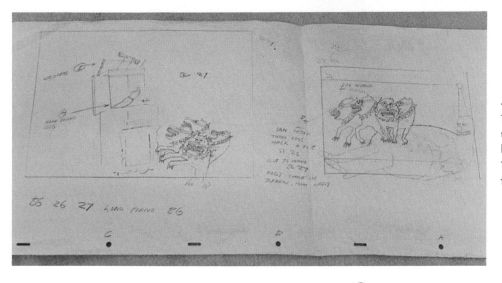

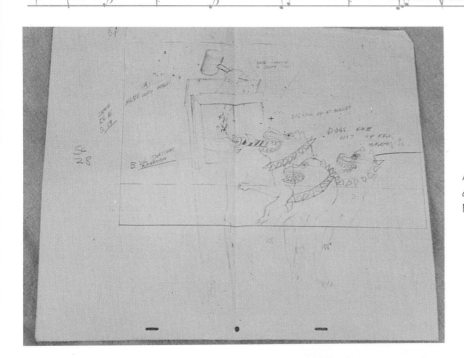

Art Animation, 1968, UK, King Features, pre-production drawings, Bulldog sequence, scene 28. Part of 3-drawing set from page 262.

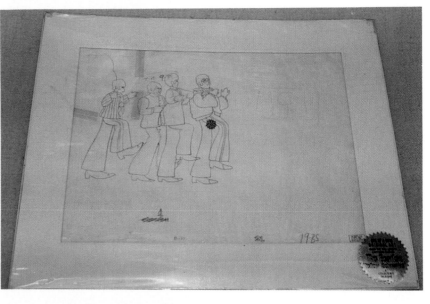

Art Animation, 1968, UK, King Features, pre-production drawings from the Yellow Submarine movie, all four Beatles. $500.00 – 600.00.

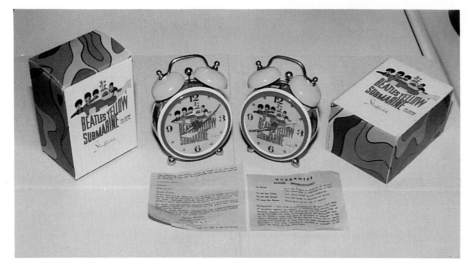

Yellow Submarine Alarm clock, 1968, manufactured by Sheffield, a rare sight. Two clocks complete with original boxes and warranty cards, $4,000.00 – 5,000.00 each. Box accounts for 50% of item's value.

Yellow Submarine banks, 1968, US, manufactured by Pride Creations, 8" tall, papier-mâché construction, rubber stopper on bottom, round and triangular stickers on bottom, originally sold in plain green boxes. Loose, $600.00 – 800.00 each; boxed, $800.00 – 1,000.00 each.

Yellow Submarine 3-ring binder and notebook set, 1968, US, manufactured by Vernon Royal. Binder, $450.00 – 600.00; large notebook, $250.00 – 350.00; small notebook, $100.00 – 200.00.

Yellow Submarine, paperback, Signet, US, 1968, $25.00 – 30.00; paperback Signet, UK, 1968, $35.00 – 40.00; hardcover, US, 1968, $75.00 – 100.00.

Yellow Submarine books, Press-out book, UK, 1968, $500.00 – 700.00; gift book, UK, 1968, $75.00 – 125.00; Sticker Fun book, UK, 1968, very rare, $800.00 – 1,000.00. All manufactured. by World Distributors, UK. A coloring book (not shown) is also known to be manufactured by this same company, $1,000.00 – 1,500.00.

Yellow Submarine books, movie premier book, US, 1968, $75.00 – 100.00; songbook, US, 1968, $100.00 – 150.00.

Yellow Submarine bookmarks, set of 6, 9" high, 1968, US. $100.00 – 150.00 set.

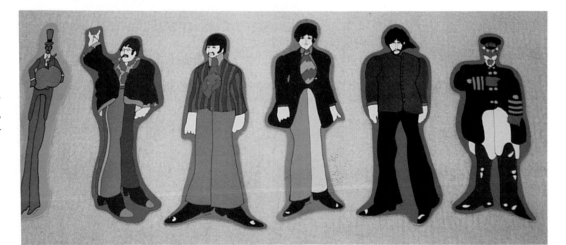

Yellow Submarine bubble gum card, set of 66, UK, Anglo Confectionery, shown with original display box. Card set, $800.00 – 1,000.00; display box, $2,000.00 – 3,000.00.

Yellow Submarine bubble gum card set, backs form poster, set of 66, UK, 1968, manufactured by Anglo Confectionery. $800.00 – 1,000.00.

Yellow Submarine bubble gum card wrappers, UK, 1968, Anglo Confectionery, one of each Beatle. $125.00 – 200.00 each.

Yellow Submarine bulletin boards, 1968, US, 7" x 23", 4 different versions, $100.00 – 150.00 each; Beatle version, $175.00 – 200.00. Values for sealed items only.

Yellow Submarine bulletin board, 2' x 2', sealed with header card, 6 different ones available, one of each Beatle, group shot, and the Yellow Submarine. Value is for sealed items. $500.00 – 700.00 each.

Yellow Submarine bulletin board, 1968, US, 2' x 2', sealed with header card, George Harrison version. $500.00 – 700.00.

Yellow Submarine buttons, various manufacturers, US, 1968 – 1980. $10.00 – 30.00 each.

Yellow Submarine calendar, 1968, US, manufactured by Western Publishing Co., with original envelope. $600.00 – 800.00. Calendar without envelope, $350.00 – 450.00.

Yellow Submarine candy cigarette box, 1968, UK, manufactured by Primrose Confectionery, with insert and one card, $250.00 – 350.00. Yellow Submarine 50-card set, UK, $250.00 – 350.00.

Cereal boxes, Rice and Wheat Honeys, manufactured by Nabisco, 1968, US. Complete box, $1,000.00 – 2,000.00. Very rare. Be aware that both boxes have been widely reproduced.

Yellow Submarine cereal box, back panel from Rice Honeys, manufactured by Nabisco, 1968, US. Complete box, $1,000.00 – 2,000.00. Rub-ons from Rice Honeys or Wheat Honeys cereal, set of 8, 1968, US. $45.00 – 60.00 per rub-on.

Yellow Submarine clothes hangers, 1968, US, manufactured by Henderson-Haggard. Loose, $150.00 – 200.00 each; set of 4 in original package, $1,000.00 – 1,500.00.

Yellow Submarine party coasters, sealed in original shrink wrap, 1968, US. $200.00 – 300.00.

Yellow Submarine comic book, 1968, US, gold key with poster, $150.00 – 200.00; *Teenset* Magazine, US, 1968, $35.00 – 50.00.

Yellow Submarine desk set, 1968, US, manufactured. by A & M Leatherline, very rare. Blotter, $2,500.00 – 3,000.00; pencil cup, $800.00 – 1,000.00; letter holder, $1,000.00 – 1,200.00; pen holder, $1,200.00 – 1,500.00; memo pad holder, $1,000.00 – 1,200.00. Other desk set items are oval desk caddy, address book, and diary.

Yellow Submarine dimensionals, 1968, US, manufactured by Craftmaster, 15" x 18" envelope, put together paper sculpture inside, "D-1 The Beatles." Values for sealed items only. $600.00 – 700.00 each. Value for assembled dimensional without envelope, $150.00 – 250.00.

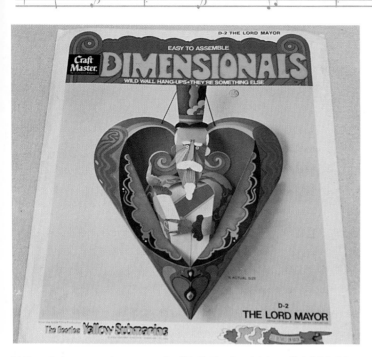

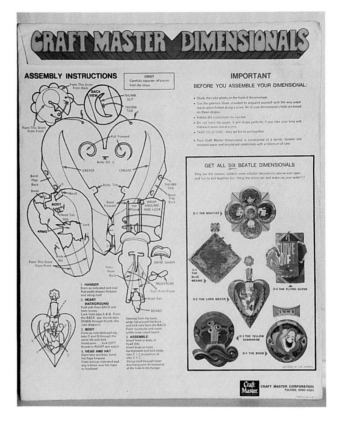

Yellow Submarine dimensionals, "D-2 The Lord Mayor." $600.00 – 700.00.

Yellow Submarine, showing back of 15" x 18" envelope for dimensionals.

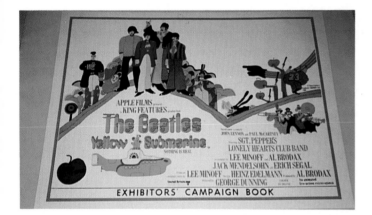

Yellow Submarine Exhibitors Campaign Book, UK, features posters, banners, and items associated with the release of the Yellow Submarine movie. $350.00 – 450.00.

Yellow Submarine store display box for glove puppets, UK, 1968, manufactured by Bellamy's, contained glove puppets which were filled with various candies. Very rare. $2,500.00 – 3,000.00.

Yellow Submarine Goebel figurines, West Germany, 1968, back-side view. See cover for front of figures. $4,000.00 – 5,000.00 each.

Yellow Submarine greeting cards, UK, 1968, rare. $50.00 – 75.00 each.

Yellow Submarine, greeting cards in boxes, 1968, US, manufactured by Sunshine Art Studios, complete set of cards with envelopes in box. Box of 15 or box of 20 styles, $300.00 – 400.00. Sunshine Art Studios also manufactured two other variations (not shown) containing 14 and 18 cards. Valued same as 15 and 20 card sets.

Yellow Submarine Halloween costume, 1968, US, manufactured by Collegeville Costumes, "The Yellow Submarine" style, costume & mask, $600.00 – 800.00; boxed, $1,200.00 – 1,800.00.

Yellow Submarine Halloween costume, 1968, US, manufactured by Collegeville Costumes, Blue Meanie Deluxe version, has flasher light in mask, rare, costume & mask. $800.00 – 1,000.00; boxed, $1,500.00 – 2,000.00.

Yellow Submarine keychains, 1968, US, manufactured by Pride Creations, rectangular set of 5, $100.00 – 150.00; round set of 6, $250.00 – 300.00.

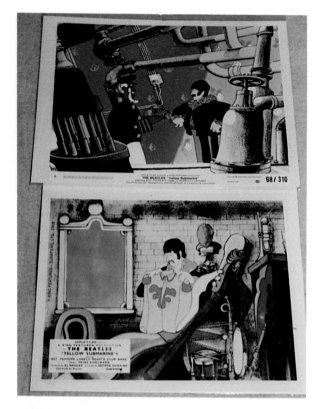

Yellow Submarine lobby cards, US, small and UK versions. $50.00 – 75.00.

Yellow Submarine lobby cards, 1968, manufactured by United Artists, set of eight cards used by theaters to promote the film. $100.00 – 150.00 each.

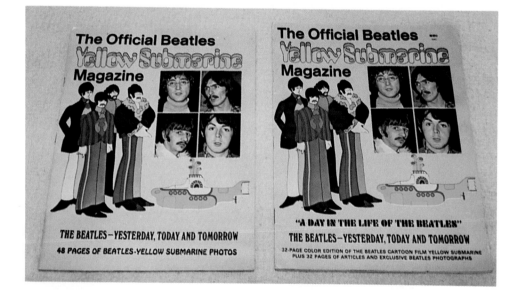

Yellow Submarine magazines, 1968, US, *The Official Beatles Yellow Submarine Magazines,* 48- and 64-page versions. $50.00 – 60.00.

Yellow Submarine, *Yale Literary Magazine,* 1968, US, $200.00 – 250.00. Heinz Edelmann autograph, designer of Yellow Submarine characters, $100.00 – 200.00.

Yellow Submarine magnetic poster game, Italy, 1968, various punch-out figures attach to metal background scene, sealed in original packaging with cardboard header card, rare. $2,000.00 – 3,000.00.

Yellow Submarine magnetic poster game (back).

Yellow Submarine mobile, 1968, US, manufactured by Sunshine Art Studios, sealed in original package. $200.00 – 250.00.

Yellow Submarine model kit, 1968, US, manufactured by Craftmaster, value for sealed model. $400.00 – 500.00.

Yellow Submarine needlepoint set, US, with colored yarns, vintage unknown. $150.00 – 200.00.

Yellow Submarine photo album, small, 1968, manufactured by A & M Leatherline, complete, $400.00 – 600.00. Photo album, large, manufactured by A & M Leatherline, US, $600.00 – 800.00. Scrapbook, manufactured by A & M Leatherline, complete with blank pages, $800.00 – 1,200.00.

Yellow Submarine postcards, 1968, US, large 10" x 14", set of six. $150.00 – 200.00.

Yellow Submarine postcards, 1968, US, set of five, 5½" x 10", rare. Set $150.00 – 200.00. Promotional version set has stories printed on the back of each postcard. $300.00 – 400.00.

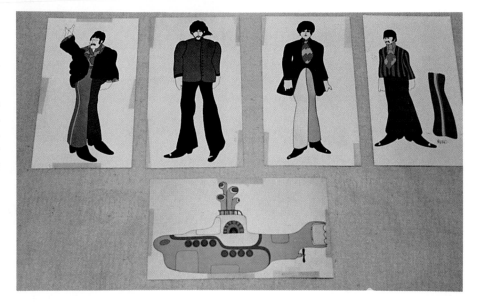

Yellow Submarine poster put-ons store display and poster put-ons, 1968, US, manufactured by Craftmaster. Display, $300.00 – 400.00; poster put-ons, $250.00 – 300.00 each.

Yellow Submarine poster put-ons, 1968, US, manufactured by Craftmaster. Box contains poster and sheet of rub-ons and a wooden stick. $250.00 – 300.00 each.

Yellow Submarine, poster, USA, one-sheet, 1968, United Artists, 27" x 41". $600.00 – 800.00. Original movie posters of the 1960s came in various sizes: half-sheet, one-sheet, three-sheets, six-sheets and 24-sheets. The one-sheet is the most popular size and commands the highest value; other sizes bring 50% – 75% of the one-sheet value.

Yellow Submarine poster, UK, one-sheet movie poster, manufactured in 1968 by United Artists. $1,000.00 – 1,500.00. This actual poster is glued to a masonite backing; it originally had an easel backing and was displayed at the opening premiere of the movie on July 17, 1968 at the London Pavilion, England

Yellow Submarine poster, Italian, 1968, one-sheet, United Artists. Beware of counterfeits. $200.00 – 300.00.

Yellow Submarine poster, 1968, German, one-sheet movie poster, manufactured by United Artists, rare. $500.00 – 600.00.

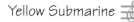

Yellow Submarine poster. US, 1968, came folded in *Eye Magazine*. $75.00 – 85.00.

Yellow Submarine poster, US, 1968, 21" x 29" mail-away poster, set of 4 different posters available. $150.00 – 200.00 each.

Yellow Submarine poster, US, 1968, 21" x 29" mail-away poster, set of 4 different posters available. $150.00 – 200.00 each.

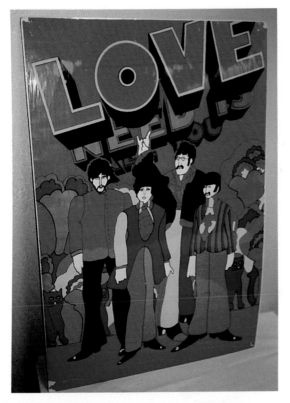

Yellow Submarine poster, black light, 1968, US, manufactured by Poster Prints, 24" x 36". $300.00 – 500.00.

Yellow Submarine poster, black light, 1969, US, manufactured by Poster Prints, 24" x 36", rare. $800.00 – 1,000.00.

Yellow Submarine puppet, 16" cloth and felt Blue Meanie hand puppet, side view. Other characters known to exist are the mini Blue Meanie and the Boob. $600.00 – 800.00.

Yellow Submarine puzzles, 1968, US, manufactured by Jay Mar, complete set of all nine different designs, small 100-piece version, 4" x 6" box. The small puzzles were not sealed like the medium and large versions. $200.00 – 250.00 each.

Yellow Submarine puzzle, 1968, US, manufactured by Jaymar, 100 pieces, medium size, 8" x 9½" box, four different variations of this size. Values for sealed puzzles only. $300.00 – 350.00 each.

Yellow Submarine puzzles, jigsaw, 1968, US, manufactured by Jaymar, 6 different styles, large size, 650 pieces, 12" x 12" box. Left: "Beatles in Pepperland," $400.00 – 500.00; right: "Blue Meanies Attack." Values for sealed puzzles only; opened puzzles are valued at 50% of the sealed prices. $400.00 – 500.00.

Yellow Submarine reel-to-reel tape, in box, 1968, US, Capitol Records, $75.00 – 100.00. Art Exhibit booklet, German, 1969, Heinz Edelmann artwork titled "Monsters, Beatles and Edelmann," rare, $200.00 – 300.00.

Yellow Submarine stationery, US, 1968, manufactured by Unicorn Creations, Beatles. $100.00 – 175.00 each.

Yellow Submarine stationery, US, 1968, manufactured by Unicorn Creations. $100.00 – 175.00 each.

Yellow Submarine stationery, US, 1968, manufactured by Unicorn Creations. $100.00 – 175.00 each.

Example of back of box of Yellow Submarine stationery. Each box contained 20 envelopes and pieces of stationery. A total of 16 different designs are known to exist.

Yellow Submarine stick-ons, 1968, US, manufactured by DAL, 9" x 12", 3 variations, Beatles, $75.00 – 100.00; others, $50.00 – 60.00. Values for sealed items only.

Yellow Submarine submarine, 1968, UK, manufactured by Corgi, metal die-cast toy, loose $250.00 – 350.00; boxed, $800.00 – 1,000.00. Pin set, set of nine, hand-painted pins, 1968, US, $75.00 – 85.00.

Yellow Submarine switchplate covers, 1968, US, set of five different styles, 6" x 12", $50.00 – 75.00 each; Beatle version, $75.00 – 100.00. Values for sealed items only.

Yellow Submarine t-shirt, 1968, UK, licensed white t-shirt with color pictures of the Beatles, rare. $500.00 – 700.00.

Yellow Submarine tie tac on card, vintage unknown, $50.00 – 75.00. Sgt. Peppers Lonely Hearts Club Band embroidered 3" patch, vintage unknown, $50.00 – 60.00.

Yellow Submarine ticket to UK world premiere, July 1968, UK, rare. $300.00 – 400.00.

Yellow Submarine theatre display for L.A. and N.Y.C. openings, 1968, 8' x 5' x 4' fiberglass display. $25,000.00 – 30,000.00.

Yellow Submarine wallpaper, Holland, very rare, 1968. One panel, $500.00 – 700.00; entire roll, $2,000.00 – 4,000.00.

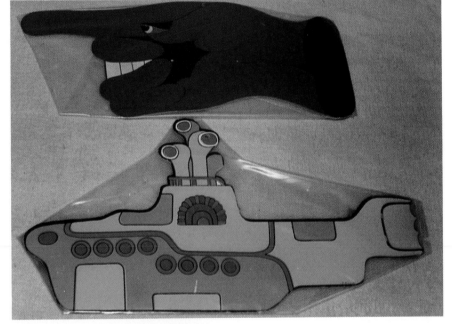

Yellow Submarine wall plaques, 1968, US, stiff cardboard. Yellow Submarine, $200.00 – 250.00; glove, $75.00 – 100.00.

Yellow Submarine, wall plaques, 1968, US, 9" x 21" black light stiff cardboard displays, one of each Beatle, slight variations exist. $100.00 – 125.00 each.

Yellow Submarine water color sets, 1968, US, manufactured by Craftmaster. Large set sealed, $250.00 – 350.00; small set sealed, $150.00 – 250.00.

Wristwatch, 1968, manufactured by Sheffield Watch Co., West Germany. This watch has been reproduced with a paper dial. Original is a painted tin litho with thick vinyl band with brass buckle and psychedelic pictures of each Beatle. There is no known Yellow Submarine specific box manufactured by Sheffield for this watch. In working condition with hang tag. $4000.00 – 6000.00.

The Banana Splits

"Tra-la-la Tra-la-la-la" was what you heard when you tuned into NBC-TV Saturday mornings from September 7, 1968 through September 5, 1970. The Banana Splits Adventure Hour was a successful rock-n-roll show featuring four costumed figures dressed as animals that performed skits in their playhouse. The show was sponsored by Kellogg's and offered several mail-in premiums including a fan club, mug and bowl set, and records. This colorful action series by Hanna-Barbera was targeted at the under 10-year-old audience.

The animals were Fleegle a dog, Drooper a lion, Bingo a gorilla, and Snorky an elephant. The Banana Splits, unlike the more abrasive musical acts that the kids' teen brothers and sisters followed, were just pure clean fun. They bumbled around their playhouse, played rock-n-roll songs, and promoted such practices as helping mom and dad, learning at school, taking out the garbage, and cleaning up. It truly was a milestone for Hanna-Barbera to include children in rock-n-roll but not deviate from moral guidelines.

Banana Splits memorabilia is becoming extremely difficult to find. Their colorful toys have long been sought after by rock-n-roll and toy collectors alike. All Splits toys are a good investment to purchase in most any condition. Since most of these items were played with by children years ago, finding Splits items in excellent to mint condition is extremely rare. This makes even the slightest grading improvement (say from fine condition, Grade 7, to an excellent condition, Grade 8) extremely favorable. Though some items are more scarce, The Banana Splits vinyl lunch box continues to be one of the most sought after and higher priced items merchandised by the group.

Art animation cel of one of the "Three Musketeers," a cartoon which appeared on the Banana Splits Show, rare. $150.00 – 200.00.

Banana band set, Larami, 1970. $35.00 – 50.00.

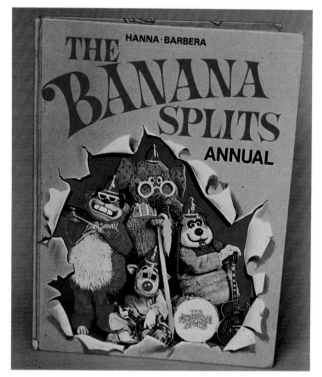

"Annual," hardcover book, 1969. $50.00 – 60.00.

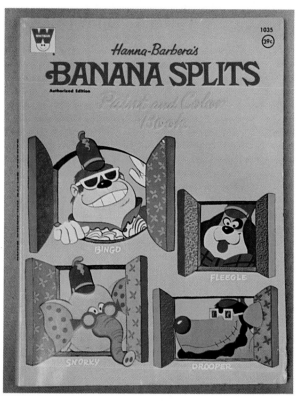

Paint and Color book, Whitman, 1969. $30.00 – 45.00.

Pinback buttons, 1972. Large, $10.00 – 15.00. Small, $40.00 – 45.00.

Catalog by H.B. Enterprises, Inc., 1970. This was sent out to TV affiliates offering Banana Splits merchandise, costumes, sets, premiums, give-aways, etc. $75.00 – 100.00. (front)

Back of H.B. Enterprises Catalog above right.

Cereal boxes from Canada by Kelloggs, 1968, US. Reproductions exist. $200.00 – 300.00

Backs of Canadian cereal boxes.

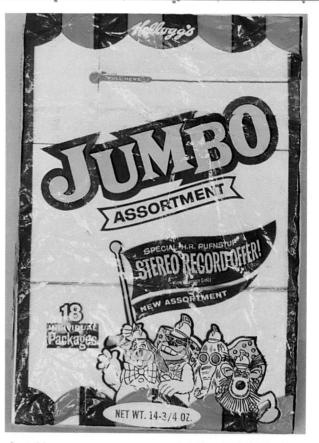

Cereal box wrapper, very rare, Kellogg's, 1968, $350.00 – 450.00.

Stamp pad set, cereal premium, 1968, rare. $250.00 – 275.00.

Erasers, cereal premium, Kellogg's, 1968. $25.00 – 30.00 each.

Sears catalog, 1969 (offering Splits merchandise).
$50.00 – 75.00.

Comic books, Gold Key, 1968 – 1970 $15.00 – 20.00 each.

17" cups, 1973. $30.00 – 40.00 each.

Dishware. Cereal bowl, $40.00 – 45.00. Flee-
gle mug, $15.00 – 20.00. Both were cereal
send-away premiums from Kellogg's, 1969.

Eraser set, 2" figures, cereal premium, Kellogg's, 1969. $40.00 – 50.00 each.

Doll, 6" rubber figure of "Fleegle," Hanna-Barbera Productions, rare. 1968. $85.00 – 125.00.

Dolls, plush figures, $60.00 – 100.00 each.

Dolls, Sutton figures, 1969. $75.00 – 100.00 each.

Doll, Sutton figure "Fleegle" in wrapper, 1969. $125.00 – 150.00.

Dolls, cloth pillow figures, 1968. Cereal send-away offer. $25.00 – 35.00 each. With wrapper, $35.00 – 45.00.

Doll, version 2 plush "Bingo" figure (lg. carnival prize), Animal Creations LTD., 1969, rare. $125.00 – 150.00.

Doll, plush "Drooper" figure (lg. carnival prize), Animal Creations, 1969. $125.00 – 150.00.

Flute set, Larami, 1969. $25.00 – 35.00.

Kut-up Kit, Larami, 1973. $25.00 – 35.00.

Handyman's Helper Set, Larami, 1970. $40.00 – 60.00.

Halloween costume, Ben Cooper, 1968. "Bingo" was the only one made. $150.00 – 200.00.

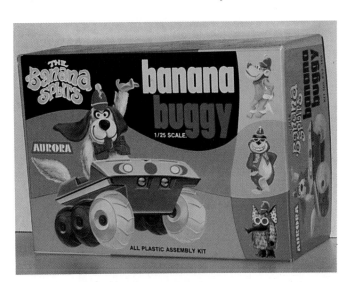

"Banana Buggy," Aurora model kit, very rare. $700.00 – 800.00.

Big wind music set, Larami, 1970. $30.00 – 40.00.

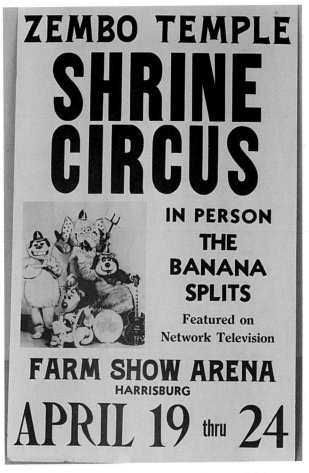

Advertisement poster from town fair in 1969, rare. $100.00 – 150.00.

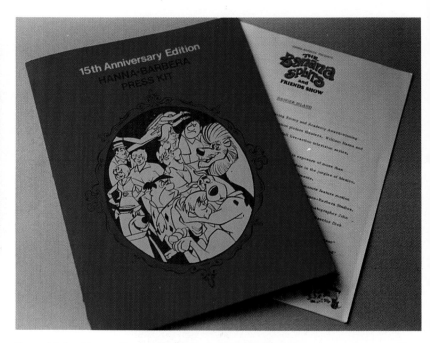

Press kit for Hanna-Barbera's 15th anniversary (includes photo of Hanna-Barbera, Banana Splits information, synopsis of shows for that season plus specials). In red folder by World Vision Dist., 1972, $175.00 – 225.00.

"Bingo" poster, cereal send-away offer from Canada, Kellogg's, 1969. $50.00 – 75.00.

Press photo of the group from 1969. Issued as b&w photo. Left to right: Bingo, Drooper, Snorky, Fleegle, $30.00 – 40.00.

Press photo of the "Sour Grape Girls," as side act on the show. The girls performed as rock-n-roll dancers. By World Vision, 1968, issued as b & w photo. $50.00 – 60.00.

Press photo for "Danger Island." Picture of Ronne Troup, daughter of jazz musician Bobby Troup, holding monkey. By World Vision Ent., issued as b&w photo, 1968. $40.00 – 50.00.

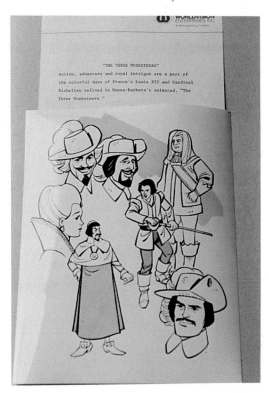

Press photo for "The Three Musketeers" by World Vision, 1968, issued as b&w photo. $45.00 – 55.00.

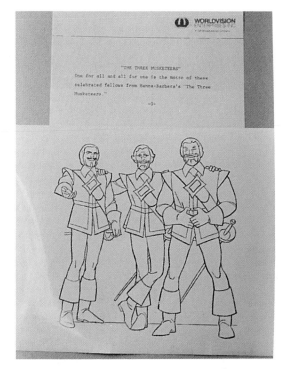

Press photo for "The Three Musketeers" cartoon which ran in the Banana Splits Comedy Hour, by World Vision Ent., 1968, issued as b&w photo. $45.00 – 55.00.

Promo press photo line drawings of each, 1968, issued as b&w photo. $30.00 – 40.00.

Promo press photo of "Bingo", 1968, issued as b & w photo. $30.00 – 40.00.

Color ad from a press kit, 1969. $50.00 – 75.00.

Plastic handpuppets (cereal premium), Kellogg's, 1968. $30.00 – 40.00 each.

Plastic handpuppets, cereal premium, Hanna-Barbera Productions, 1968. $30.00 – 40.00 each.

Frame tray puzzles, Whitman, 1969. $15.00 – 20.00 each.

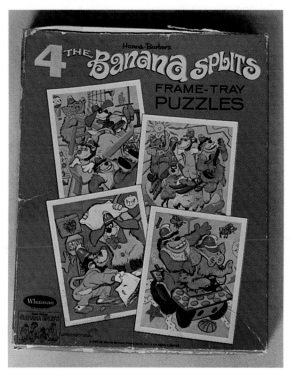

Frame tray puzzle box, Whitman, 1969, $40.00 – 50.00 (empty).

Jigsaw puzzle, Whitman, 1970. $40.00 – 50.00.

Slide puzzle, Roalex, 1968. $60.00 – 70.00.

45 RPM record, cereal send-away offer, by Decca, 1969. $25.00 – 30.00.

45 RPM record, cereal send-away offer, Decca, 1969. $25.00 – 30.00.

Record album, $75.00 – 100.00. Cassette, $20.00 – 30.00. Decca, 1968.

School tablet, 8" x 10", by Westab, 1968, $40.00 – 50.00.

Switch plate cover, King's Island, 1970. $35.00 – 45.00.

Birthday tablecloth, $75.00 – 85.00. Party cup set, $50.00 – 60.00. Both by Beach Productions, 1969.

Tambourines. Left: header card, $60.00 – 70.00. Right: blister card, $75.00 – 85.00. Both by Larami, 1973.

Tattoo gumball display card, Fleer, 1969. $40.00 – 50.00.

The Chipmunks

Alvin, Theodore, and Simon became popular in 1958 when their hit, "The Chipmunk Song" spent four weeks at the number one position. This nostalgic Christmas song was just the beginning of The Chipmunks' popularity. From 1958 – 1962 the group charted a total of eight Top 40 entries, equal to such heavy hitters as The Doors. Though their album sales didn't compare, their popularity did and continues today.

Through their creator's success with a previous number one single, "Witch Doctor", in April of 1958, Ross Bagdasarian (using the name David Seville) began experimenting with sound. By speeding up vocal tracks, The Chipmunks were born. For the first time in history, animals were seen playing rock-n-roll. The Chipmunks paved the way for such acts as The Banana Splits and The Bugaloos.

With the success of the songs, CBS-TV aired a prime time animated series entitled "The Alvin Show" on October 14, 1961. The original show ran through September 12, 1962, for a total of 26 episodes. The show hit pay-dirt with the kids. The Chipmunks have stood the test of time and are certainly a part of our American history.

Many items have been marketed for the Chipmunks and in particular for their leader Alvin. Chipmunk toys were first produced in the late 1950s. The early Chipmunk figures were very unlike the figures we see today. The first figures resembled real-life chipmunks with a large letter representing their name monogrammed on their shirts. As their popularity increased, the figures transformed into cuter characters, ones that children could relate to better. Another transition appeared in 1983 with the addition of other characters including the Chipettes. A final change occurred in the late 1980s when the three main characters took on a more youthful appearance.

Chipmunks memorabilia is available, fun, and collectible. Most of the early merchandise (pre-1970) is of substantial value today. The vinyl lunch kit produced in 1962 is perhaps the most highly desired of all The Chipmunks' collectibles. The challenging aspect of collecting Chipmunk memorabilia is that since so many items were produced, it's nearly impossible to discover them all. Even serious Chipmunk collectors will constantly find items that they never knew existed.

Chipmunks "The TV Chipmunks" book, Random House, 1984. $5.00 – 8.00.

Chipmunks bandages, Dayton-Hudson, 1990. $5.00 – 8.00.

Chipmunks tote bag, Dayton-Hudson, 1984. $5.00 – 10.00.

Chipmunks Christmas stocking, unknown manufacturer, 1964. $35.00 – 55.00.

Chipmunks Christmas Stocking, unknown manufacturer, 1963. $35.00 – 55.00.

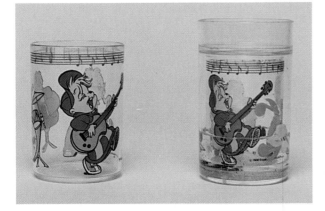

Chipmunks plastic mug, Dayton-Hudson, 1990. $10.00 – 15.00.

Chipmunks plastic cup, $5.00 – 10.00; Dayton-Hudson, 1990. plastic tumbler, $5.00 – 10.00.

Chipmunks (pre-cartoon) dishware. Plate, $45.00 – 55.00; mug, $35.00 – 45.00; bowl, $45.00 – 55.00.

Chipmunks dishware. Plate, $10.00 – 15.00; bowl, Dayton-Hudson, 1984. $10.00 – 15.00.

Chipmunks doll, Alvin squeeze toy, unknown manufacturer, 1964. $35.00 – 45.00.

Chipmunks (pre-cartoon) large stuffed Alvin Doll, Timely Toys, 1960. $85.00 – 95.00.

Chipmunks dolls, Poseable Play Pals, Ideal, 1984. $5.00 – 8.00 each.

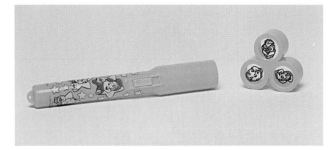

Chipmunks flashlight (premium), Delmonte, 1991, produced as a send-away item. $25.00 – 30.00.

Chipmunks game, Curtain Call Theater, Ideal, 1984, U.S. $40.00 – 50.00.

Chipmunks (pre-cartoon), "Acorn Hunt" game, Hasbro, 1960. $75.00 – 100.00.

Chipmunks glasses, 1985. $5.00 – 6.00 each.

Chipmunks jigsaw puzzle 63 pcs., 1984. $5.00 – 8.00.

Chipmunks (pre-cartoon), loot box, $55.00 – 65.00; wallet, $40.00 – 50.00; song tote, $100.00 – 150.00. All by Monarch Music Co., 1959.

Chipmunks Alvin handpuppet 9", Dayton-Hudson, 1990. $10.00 – 12.00.

Chipmunks "Soaky" bubble bath figures, Colgate Palmolive, 1963. $25.00 – 35.00.

Chipmunks spoon & fork set, Dayton-Hudson, 1990. $10.00 – 15.00.

Chipmunks sticker pack, Ambassador, 1984. $5.00 – 8.00.

Chipmunks walkie-talkie, Helm Toy Company, 1985. $10.00 – 15.00.

Lunchboxes

What was contained inside the lunchbox wasn't nearly as important to the owner as who was pictured on the box itself. Lunchboxes represented a genuine way for a youngster to show off his or her hero to the world each and every day. More importantly, this was the best way to swear allegiance to their idols.

Rock-n-roll lunchboxes were targeted at young audiences beginning in the early 1960s. These boxes were usually produced by large lunchbox manufacturers such as Aladdin or Thermos. Other lesser known companies produced boxes as well which sometimes makes them worth even greater values. Lunchboxes were made of steel, vinyl covered cardboard or plastic. In addition to the standard square type box was the vinyl brunch-bag. Brunch-bags are highly sought after due to their scarcity and limited production. Vinyl boxes and brunch-bags are hard to find. Excellent to mint condition examples are even harder to locate. The rapid deterioration of the cardboard liner inside (which shaped them) and vinyl tears in the box are commonplace with these boxes.

The most valuable of all lunchboxes continue to be The Beatles Kaboodle Kits which were created for Beatles fans in America by Standard Plastic Products (SPP). The Beatles Kaboodle Kits were produced in a variety of colors; some of these colors are scarcer than others and prices reflect this. These kits have nearly disappeared from circulation entirely (in any condition). Many of these are in personal collections and regarded as rare, highly collectible and valuable.

Other metal and vinyl lunchboxes and brunch-bags continue to climb in value to new heights. A box's condition and its nostalgic value each play a key role in its value. Plastic boxes also continue to gain popularity and value in today's market.

The Archies metal lunchbox, Aladdin, 1969. Box $65.00 – 95.00; thermos (plastic with glass liner), $20.00 – 35.00.

The Banana Splits, Thermos, 1969. Box (vinyl), $300.00 – 400.00; thermos (metal), $100.00 – 150.00.

The Beatles, a sampling of the different lunchboxes of the 1960s.

The Beatles lunchboxes, manufactured by AirFlite, 1964, US, vinyl. Light blue, $700.00 – 1,000.00; black, $1,000.00 – 1,500.00; red, $700.00 – 1,000.00. Not shown, brown, $1,200.00 – 1,600.00, rare. Note: Brown case has no handle, and was originally sold as a makeup case.

Lunchbox, 1965, US, manufactured by Aladdin, blue vinyl brunch-bagwith black strap, zippered top. Originally sold with a red plaid generic thermos (not the Beatles thermos, as most believe). $500.00 – 700.00.

The Beatles, Vinyl Kaboodle Kit, manufactured by Standard Plastic Products (SPP), 1964, US. Eight known colors: yellow, $800.00 – 1,000.00, dark blue, $800.00 – 1,000.00, light blue, $800.00 – 1,000.00, beige, $800.00 – 1,000.00, peach, $1,000.00 – 1,200.00, red, $1,000.00 – 1,200.00, hot pink, $1,200.00 – 1,500.00, and lavender $1,200.00 – 1,500.00.

The Beatles metal lunchbox. Aladdin, 1965. Box, $800.00 – 1,200.00; thermos, extremely hard to find in true near mint condition. $200.00 – 300.00.

The Beatles, Yellow Submarine lunchbox and thermos, 1968, US, manufactured by Thermos. Lunchbox, $1,000.00 – 1,400.00; thermos, extremely hard to fine in true near mint condition. $300.00 – 400.00.

Bugaloos metal lunchbox, Aladdin, 1971. $65.00 – 100.00; thermos (plastic), $35.00 – 55.00.

The Bee Gees lunchboxes, $50.00 – 60.00, each; thermos, $10.00 – 15.00, by Thermos, 1978. Bottom center box shows reverse of other three boxes.

Chipmunks thermos and lunchbox. Thermos, 1963. Thermos, $40.00 – 60.00; lunchbox, $250.00 – 350.00.

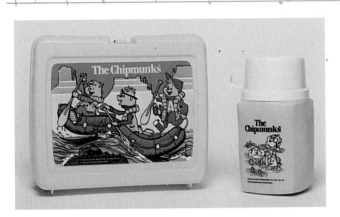

Chipmunks plastic lunchbox, Thermos, 1984. $10.00 – 15.00; plastic thermox, $5.00 – 8.00.

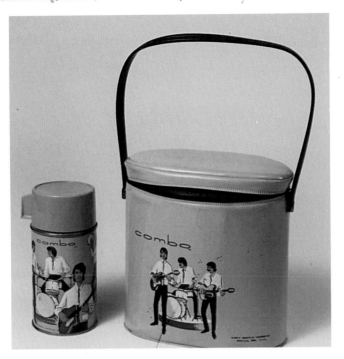

Combo brunch-bag, Aladdin, 1967, rare. $400.00 – 500.00; thermos, $50.00 – 100.00.

Disco metal lunchbox, 1979. $50.00 – 75.00; thermos (plastic), $25.00 – 35.00.

Disco Fever metal lunchbox, Thermos, 1980. $50.00 – 75.00; thermos (plastic), $25.00 – 35.00.

Donnie & Marie vinyl brunch-bags by Aladdin. Long hair (1976), $100.00 – 150.00; thermos (plastic), $20.00 – 30.00. Short hair (1977), $100.00 – 150.00; thermos (plastic), $20.00 – 30.00.

The Osmonds metal lunchbox, $65.00 – 95.00; thermos (plastic), 2 different types each, $20.00 – 35.00, by Aladdin, 1973.

Go Go vinyl lunchbox, $175.00 – 225.00; thermos (metal), $45.00 – 60.00, by Aladdin, 1966.

Go Go vinyl brunchbag, $175.00 – 225.00; thermos (metal), $45.00 – 60.00, by Aladdin, 1966.

Hammer "Hammerman" thermos, $5.00 – 10.00; lunchbox, $20.00 – 25.00, from short-lived Saturday morning cartoon show, 1991.

KISS metal lunchbox, thermos, US, 1977. $150.00 – 200.00; thermos (plastic), $25.00 – 45.00.

The Monkees plastic lunchbox kit from Canada, Raybert products 1967, $150.00 – 225.00; thermos, $40.00 – 65.00.

New Kids On The Block lunchbox, $10.00 – 15.00 each; thermos, $5.00 – 10.00 each. Photo box 1990, cartoon box, 1991. Both produced by Thermos.

The Partridge Family metal lunchbox, Thermos, 1971. $65.00 – 95.00; plastic thermos, $25.00 – 35.00; metal thermos, $30.00 – 45.00.

Pussycats vinyl brunch-bag, Aladdin, 1968. $175.00 – 225.00; thermos (plastic), $40.00 – 50.00.

Pussycats vinyl lunchbox, Aladdin, 1968. $125.00 – 175.00; thermos, $45.00 – 65.00.

Shindig vinyl lunchbox, by R.D. Industries, 1960s, rare. $300.00 – 350.00.

Bobby Sherman lunchbox, Thermos, 1972. $60.00 – 80.00; thermos, $25.00 – 50.00.

Reflections
of
Collections

Vintage equipment

Vintage store signs

Vintage store signs

Beatles, Yeah, Yeah, Yeah

Elvis

Beatles

Schroeder's ANTIQUES Price Guide

. . . is the #1 bestselling antiques & collectibles value guide on the market today, and here's why . . .

• *More than 450 advisors, well-known dealers, and top-notch collectors work together with our editors to bring you accurate information regarding pricing and identification.*

• *More than 45,000 items in almost 550 categories are listed along with hundreds of sharp original photos that illustrate not only the rare and unusual, but the common, popular collectibles as well.*

• *Each large close-up shot shows important details clearly. Every subject is represented with histories and background information, a feature not found in any of our competitors' publications.*

• *Our editors keep abreast of newly developing trends, often adding several new categories a year as the need arises.*

8½ x 11, 608 Pages, $12.95

If it merits the interest of today's collector, you'll find it in *Schroeder's*. And you can feel confident that the information we publish is up to date and accurate. Our advisors thoroughly check each category to spot inconsistencies, listings that may not be entirely reflective of market dealings, and lines too vague to be of merit. Only the best of the lot remains for publication.

Without doubt, you'll find
SCHROEDER'S ANTIQUES PRICE GUIDE
the only one to buy for
reliable information and values.

COLLECTOR BOOKS
A Division of Schroeder Publishing Co., Inc.